FOREIGN LANGUAGES CONVERSATION

NIRANJAN JHA SHOWMAN

FRENCH

GERMAN

SPANISH

ENGLISH

Cromosys Publication

FOREIGN
LANGUAGES
CONVERSATION

NIRANJAN JHA SHOWMAN

Founder - Niranjan Jha Showman
cromosys®
Corporation
Education and Technology Research Center
Patankar Park, Nallasopara (W), Mumbai. +91-9561450045
Education, Technology, Publication, Healthcare, Newsmedia, Realtor, Filmmaking
www.facebook.com/cromosys

+91-9561450045
Learn Advanced Skills
And Get Job Instantly
GERMAN
Python
FRENCH
C++
SPANISH
Java
ENGLISH
HTML5
RUSSIAN
CSS
JavaScript
Cromosys
Education and Technology Research Center
Nallasopara (W), Mumbai

Learn Web Programming

Demo-Class Free

HTML

CSS

React

JavaScript

Typescript

Bootstrap

Cromosys
20 Years of Experience
Nallasopara (W), Mumbai
+91-9561450045

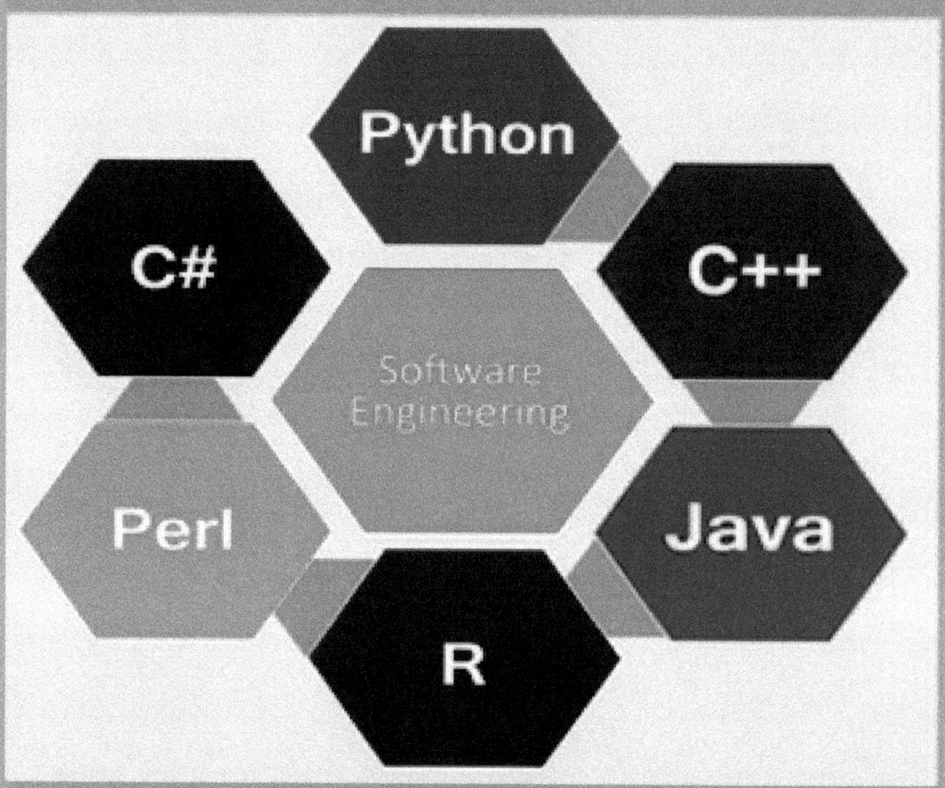
+91-9561450045
Learn Software Engineering
Demo-Class Free
Python
C#
C++
Software
Engineering
Perl
Java
R
Cromosys
20 Years of Experience
Nallasopara (W), Mumbai
+91-9561450045

25 Years of Experience
Learn Visual Multimedia
Animation VFX
Movie Editing
Game Development
Cromosys
+91-9561450045
Education and Technology Research Center
Nallasopara (W), Mumbai
www.facebook.com/cromosys

Jobs Available
For Candidates Who Know

German
French
Spanish

Vacancy in Germany, France, Spain

For Hospitality, Engineering, IT Sector
With Free Visa, Airfare and Accommodation

Cromosys
Education and Technology Research Centre
Nallasopara (W), Mumbai
+91-9561450045
20 Years of Experience

+91-9561450045
Foreign Languages Institute
German, French, Spanish
Basic and Advanced - All Levels
3 x 6 = 18 Courses
FRANCHISE
Business Offer
Teaching Materials Provided
We have 1 Million Students Globally
Great Income Assured
Global Exposure
Cromosys
20 Years of Experience
Nallasopara (W), Mumbai
+91-9561450045

Cromosys Publication

Foreign Languages Conversation

French – Spanish – German – English

Niranjan Jha Showman

"Education taken with zeal educes to success."
~Niranjan Showman

Preface

In this new world, after you do the basic course of French, Spanish or German, you feel the necessity of increasing your conversational skill. The basic course teaches you the grammar and conjugation of a language, but does not teach you how to develop your speaking ability. And when you try to frame sentences, either you go very slowly or you are too late. Considering this difficulty of foreign languages learners across the world, I have written this book to help you gain spoken knowledge of French, Spanish or German language. This book helps you speak any one of the three languages with a good flow.

This Foreign Languages Conversation book of Cromosys Publication is an optimal quality guide to the beginners as well as advanced learners. French, Spanish or German is of great demand after English because it is widely spoken in many European countries America and Canada. Language is the pillar of human origin and evolution, and so, even many other languages of the world died in this century, but these three languages are still surviving and flourishing because of their strong root in human culture and civilization. Moreover, these languages are the creator of English which is already said by the father of English Literature Geoffrey Chaucer, then William Wordsworth and William Shakespeare.

This book is unmatchable and unique of its kind that guarantees your success. The lessons and study materials exclusively designed are based on my fifteen years of research in linguistic field. The text and audio suggestions magnificently powerful to bring you into educational light. Whether your intention is to travel abroad or plunge deep into your research, if you need to learn a language, then one among these three is the best choice. Having been teaching these languages for twenty years globally with high exposure, and being able to understand linguistic science, I would like to assure you that this language is easy to learn in just one moth of daily practice. And once learnt, with your sharpened bilingual ability, you can make your way of success without any hindrance. After you start the lesson of this book, you don't need to worry about anything but just follow each and everything carefully. Don't procrastinate, over-confide or give up. You are going to do the most beautiful thing for yourself, so be bold enough to complete all the lessons. The sentence constructions of these languages are similar to English. The only thing for which your effort has to be hard enough is its pronunciation, for which I have suggested to use online support. Only you have to practice over it as everything is explained properly.

The significance of this book is that it is dynamic, systemic and blissful with abundance of pure and perfect set of rules that took a decade of time in preparation. One alone, being immaturely suggested, spend ages in watching movies and listening to the audio which help them to imitate a little but not learn what in actual sense it is, and their never-ending process of Picasso Adventure collects some scattered information which is unworthy to learning a foreign language. And the aspirants get lost in wilderness. I have designed this book with proper set of lessons to make you start your adventure sitting at home beginning after basic. This book is highly useful for the people working in communication based industry, media houses, entertainment world, and for those who are teachers, writers, researchers and students. And definitely for those who love languages.

Cromosys, our education and technology research center, saving human efforts from being wasted, is to teach you this language as good as possible. The world has brought enormous opportunity to foreign language speakers irrespective of their geographical boundaries. Having been teaching this language for several years, I have come across the numerous rules which I have elaborated in this book. Our path-breaking pioneer training institute for Languages and Computer Science, is committed to enlightening human mind with educational endeavors, and we are doing the same for last successful twenty years. I believe I have done all I could to make this book useful to you, and not only hopeful but I am sure that your success is in your hand now because this book will take you miles ahead in your expectation. We always respect the views and comments of readers, so for any communication with regards to assistance, enquiry or collaboration, we are always there at your reach as it helps us improve our quality.

This is a book for learning conversation in French, Spanish, German language through English. We advise to use and learn this conversation of ANY ONE language (not all at a time), and also when you have completed or about to complete your basic learning in any one of these foreign languages from a standard institute. Please be advised that without having a basic knowledge of a foreign language, understanding this conversation is impossible. You need to write English and the foreign language (one) translation first in your notebook, and then, listen to the audio from Google Translate and repeat it until your pronunciation gets clear. It is also important that you need to do only one lesson in a day because making haste may lead to illusion and frustration.

If you want to learn the basic of French, Spanish or German, then try to find those books on Amazon authored by me, titled – Teach Yourself French, Teach Yourself Spanish, and Teach Yourself German. If you wish to do A1, A2 or more advanced course in these foreign language, you can contact us for online or offline class as we are always there to help you.

Niranjan Jha Showman
Trainer, Author Physician, Entrepreneur, Filmmaker, Activist
Founder of Cromosys Corporation
facebook.com/cromosys
+91-9561450045
cromosys@yahoo.com
Nallasopara (W), Mumbai, India

Other books by the same author: -
English Voice Accent and Pronunciation
Teach Yourself German
Teach Yourself French
Teach Yourself Spanish
Be millionaire like me
Dynamic Grammar of English
Teach Yourself HTML5
Teach Yourself 3ds Max
Teach Yourself Autodesk Maya

Cromosys Corporation
Education and Technology Research Center
Education, Technology, Publication, Healthcare, Realtor, Filmmaking
facebook.com/cromosys
+91-9561450045
cromosys@yahoo.com
Nallasopara (W), Mumbai, India

About the Author

Niranjan Jha Showman
Trainer, Author, Physician, Entrepreneur, Filmmaker, Activist

Niranjan Jha Showman is a Language Scientist and Technical Researcher. He is the Award Winning author of more than fifty educational and fictional books at Amazon. He is one of the great-grandsons of the first President of India Dr. Rajendra Prasad. He is a Public Figure, and the globally - renowned Languages Trainer of French, Spanish, and German from past twenty years. Niranjan Jha Showman is an Entrepreneur and also works as a Filmmaker in India. Being the founder and owner of Cromosys Corporation - a company located in Mumbai, India, his company is excelling in the fields of Education, Technology, Publication, Newsmedia, Realtors, Banking, and Cinemascope from past fifteen years.

Niranjan Jha Showman's good-seller educational books and novels are appreciated worldwide. He has more than one million eBook buyers online, and more than one million learners are connected to him globally. One of his novels is critically acclaimed. He is the trainer of French, Spanish, German, English Voice and Accent, and Advanced Computer Education. He is also a political activist in India.

Niranjan Jha Showman is the man who came from rags to riches, he who knows how to turn the table, and he, whom you call the man of Midas-touch. He has observed lives from the Pandora of monkeys to the sanctuary of monks, not only down-to-earth but down-to-grave. He is a B. Com. graduate, and B. Ed. from Delhi University, and diploma holder in French, Spanish and German from America. You can watch his songs, movies, educational videos and many more things by typing "Niranjan Jha Showman" in Google.

Niranjan Jha Showman
+91-9561450045
cromosys@yahoo.com
Mumbai, India
facebook.com/cromosys

Statutory

This book with its content is the registered property of the author Niranjan Jha Showman.
The author and his Cromosys Publication holds all necessary rights of this book.
The copyright certificate of this book is attached at the end of this book.

This book is a copyright and its content is the registered property of the author Niranjan Jha Showman. The author and his Cromosys Publication holds all necessary rights of this book. All the writing works that include all the educational, non-educational books, novels, and articles of the writer Niranjan Jha Showman, are the registered content under MAHENG12112/13/1/2009-TC and the endorsement no. 3244 28/5/2009 with the Ministry of Information and Broadcasting, Govt. of India. Any plagiarism in this regard will attract strict legal action. Any further publication or production of any of his books requires his written permission. The copyright certificate of this book is attached at the end of this book.

Lesson 1

This is a book for learning conversation in French, Spanish, and German through English. We advise to use and learn this conversation of ANY ONE language, not all the three. And keep in mind that you can understand the conversation only when you have completed the basic course or you are about to complete from a standard institute. Please be advised that without having a basic knowledge of a foreign language, understanding this conversation is impossible.

We strongly suggest you to copy the text of a foreign language in Google Translate and listen to the audio of it carefully using earphone. You need to write English and the foreign language (one) translation first in your notebook, and then, listen to the audio from Google Translate and speak back until your pronunciation gets clear. It is also important that you need to do only one lesson in a day because making haste will lead to illusion and frustration.

Greeting

A: Good morning.

French: Bonjour.
Spanish: Buenos dias.
German: Guten Morgen.

B: Hello.

French: Salut.
Spanish: Hola.
German: Hallo.

A: How are you?

French: Comment vas-tu?
Spanish: ¿Cómo estás?
German: Wie geht es dir?

B: I am fine. And you?

French: Je vais bien. Et toi?
Spanish: Estoy bien. ¿Y tú?
German: Ich bin ok. Und Sie?

A: I am good. Thank you for asking.

French: Je vais bien. Merci de demander.
Spanish: Estoy bien. Gracias por preguntar.
German: Ich bin gut. Danke für die Nachfrage.

B: Welcome.

French: Bienvenue.
Spanish: Bienvenidas.
German: Herzlich willkommen.

A: I greet you.

        French: Je vous salue.
        Spanish: Te saludo.
        German: Ich grüße euch.

B: Me too.

        French: Moi aussi.
        Spanish: Yo también.
        German: Ich auch.

A: I am glad to see you.

        French: Je suis content de te voir.
        Spanish: Estoy feliz de verte.
        German: Ich bin froh, dich zu sehen.

B: It is my pleasure.

        French: Avec plaisir.
        Spanish: Es un placer.
        German: Es ist mir ein Vergnügen.

A: Bye Bye!

        French: Bye Bye!
        Spanish: ¡Adiós!
        German: Tschüss!

It is important to notice that greeting in these languages are different from English. In English, we greet as per time, but in French and Spanish, we greet for the entire day. The pronunciation of French: Bonjour is not as easily expected. It has different pronunciation that you can understand only after you complete the basic course of French.

In Spanish: Hola, the 'h' letter is silent, so make sure you pronounce the word correctly. In French: Comment allez vous, some letters are silent, and the sentence is pronounced having all the three words connected. This is the beauty of French, so you can understand this trick after you are thorough with basic pronunciation of French.

Exercise
Do oral translation of these sentences in your learning language.

It is my pleasure.
I am glad to see you.
I greet you.
Good morning.
How are you?
Bye Bye!

Lesson 2

This second lesson is about introduction of two persons when they meet each other. In this lesson, you learn how to ask questions and answer when you meet someone for the first time. If possible, invite a friend to participate in this conversation a A, and you will speak as B. This kind of practice will help you gain speed in your speaking with natural tone.

To check how correct your foreign language pronunciation is, you need to enable Internet connection to your computer or cellphone. Then open Google Translate, select a language on left – for example French, and press the mic button in the same box. Then you need to speak in French and check whether Google Translate types it correctly. If it types the same what you speak, that means your pronunciation is perfect. In case it does not, you need to learn correct pronunciation by typing the word and listening to the pronunciation using earphone. Or you may need to look at the pronunciation lessons you are taught by your teacher in your basic course.

Introduction

A: What is your name?

    French: Quel est ton nom?
    Spanish: ¿Cuál es su nombre?
    German: Wie heißen Sie?

B: My name is Martin.

    French: Mon nom est Martin.
    Spanish: Mi nombre es Martin.
    German: Ich heiße Martin.

A: How are you doing today?

    French: Comment ça va aujourd'hui?
    Spanish: ¿Cómo estás hoy?
    German: Wie geht es dir heute?

B: I am doing well.

    French: Je me débrouille bien.
    Spanish: Lo estoy haciendo bien.
    German: Mir geht es gut.

A: Where do you live?

    French: Où habites-tu?
    Spanish: ¿Dónde vive?
    German: Wo wohnen Sie?

B: I live in India.

    French: Je vis en Inde.
    Spanish: Yo vivo en India.
    German: Ich lebe in Indien.

A: Where do you work?

> French: Où travaillez-vous?
> Spanish: ¿Dónde trabajas?
> German: Wo arbeitest du?

B: I work in a school.

> French: Je travaille dans une école.
> Spanish: Yo trabajo en una escuela.
> German: Ich arbeite in einer Schule.

A: What is your salary?

> French: Quel est ton salaire?
> Spanish: ¿Cuál es tu salario?
> German: Was ist Ihr Gehalt?

B: My salary is twenty thousand.

> French: Mon salaire est de vingt mille.
> Spanish: Mi salario es de veinte mil.
> German: Mein Gehalt beträgt zwanzigtausend.

A: Take care!

> French: Prends soin!
> Spanish: ¡Cuídate!
> German: Pass auf!

B: See you again.

> French: À la prochaine.
> Spanish: Hasta luego.
> German: Wir sehen uns wieder.

Words in a foreign language may look similar to English but the pronunciations are quite different and sometimes strange. Do not try to imitate the pronunciation of a language without having the proper knowledge of it otherwise it leads to ridicule.

Exercise
Do oral translation of these sentences in your learning language.

I greet you.
Good morning.
How are you doing today?
Where do you live?
I work in a school.
Welcome.
See you again.

Lesson 3

Being able to speak, read and write swiftly and smoothly is what defines being fluent in a language. Theoretically speaking, fluency is an essential part of the whole process of language learning and is almost always a top priority for learners. Sociologists stress the significance of the first few seconds when building social ties – our fluency, therefore, can make or break potential friendships or business deals.

To build and improve your language fluency, here are 15 very effective tips to get you on your way:

1.   **Perfect Your Pronunciation**: Good pronunciation is essentially the most important element for speaking and understanding a language. The more you practice, the better your pronunciation will become over time. After all, practice makes better! Tip: Watch foreign movies with subtitles to listen and understand the pronunciation of words & phrases as spoken by a native speaker!

2.   **Select Words Carefully**: When speaking, your choice of vocabulary impacts the message, its context, and its pronunciation. Choosing words you're comfortable with when conversing will help improve your language proficiency. Therefore, try to select each word carefully and deliberately, keeping the message of your sentence in mind.

3.   **Read**: Expanding your vocabulary improves your articulation and language fluency. When you understand how sentences are structured, speaking is not as challenging as it may seem. Additionally, learning new words is fairly easy! You can start the process by simply learning the foreign language words of things or places that are part of your daily life and ease into the language. Tip: Paired reading with an experienced reader helps a lot!

4.   **Write**: The more you write, the better you comprehend and the more fluent you become. Writing will help you understand and become familiar with the language. Don't forget that fluency comes through practice, and writing is a key part of learning a language thoroughly.

Meeting

A: Excuse me.

    French: Pardon.
    Spanish: Perdóneme.
    German: Entschuldigen.

B: Yes. Tell me.

    French: Oui. Dis-moi.
    Spanish: Si. Dime.
    German: Ja. Sag mir.

A: Can I ask you a question?

    French: Puis-je vous poser une question?
    Spanish: ¿Puedo hacerte una pregunta?
    German: Kann ich dir eine Frage stellen?

B: With pleasure.

    French: Avec plaisir.
    Spanish: Con mucho gusto.
    German: Mit Vergnügen.

A: What place is it?

    French: C'est quel endroit?
    Spanish: ¿Qué lugar es?
    German: Welcher Ort ist es?

B: It is a theatre.

    French: C'est un théâtre.
    Spanish: Es un teatro.
    German: Es ist ein Theater.

A: I want to watch a movie.

    French: Je veux regarder un film.
    Spanish: Quiero ver una película.
    German: Ich möchte einen Film gucken.

B: Very good.

    French: Très bon.
    Spanish: Muy buena.
    German: Sehr gut.

5. **Listen, Listen, and Listen**: The more you listen to the language you are learning, the more familiar you become about using appropriate words according to the situation you're in.

6. **Practice Long Speeches**: Using long speeches and recording them at the same time will enable you to gauge fluency in the language you are learning and come back to it at a later time for review. This also improves confidence while communicating in the language you are learning.

7. **Examine Unique Characteristics of the Language**: Each language has various unique features about it. Unlocking these is crucial to being a fluent language speaker because it allows you to be aware of where and how to put stress in a sentence or a word, especially as these nuances differ from language to language, and from culture to culture.

Exercise
Do oral translation of these sentences in your learning language.

What place is it?
It is a theatre.
Where do you live?
I work in a school.
Can I ask you a question?
With pleasure.
Very good.

Lesson 4

One of the fastest routes to fluency is finding a language exchange partner. Your language buddy can be a native speaker or your classmate. Collaborating with them will help build confidence in learning the language. Simple corrections on pronunciation, sentence structure and vocabulary can be noted and corrected to help you improve and become a fluent speaker.

8. **Communicate with Yourself**: It may feel a little strange but communicating with yourself can help in evaluating if the tips are working or not. Self-directed learning helps you evaluate your own skills and make corrections prior to venturing into a formal or professional communication. Tip: Read out loud to improve verbal fluency.

9. **Travel**: Although this may be a costly, but traveling to areas where your target language is spoken gives a different take on learning the language. For example, roaming the streets of Venice or keeping up with fast-paced Tokyo will enrich your Italian and Japanese learning experience in more ways than one.

10. **Using Technology to Assist Learning**: Technology is a valuable tool in achieving foreign language fluency today. Whether it's a phone application with audio tutorials to practice your pronunciation or interactive resources & games to enhance your vocabulary, technology is essential for learning a foreign language today.

11. **Imitate other Fluent Speakers**: If you're not sure how to pronounce a word, observing native or fluent speakers can be a great guide. Imitating them and learning from their mannerisms will help you become proficient as well as motivate you to learn more.

12. **Learn in a Classroom**: Classrooms are considered to be an effective learning environment for students across the world. Language fluency can also be improved by actively participating in the classroom, and practicing the accent and pronunciation of words and phrases. Additionally, conversations among peers in the classroom help develop your skills further.

Time

A: What time is it?

        French: Quelle heure est-il?
        Spanish: ¿Qué hora es?
        German: Wie spät ist es?

B: It is five thirty.

        French: Il est cinq heures trente.
        Spanish: Son las cinco y media.
        German: Es ist fünf Uhr dreißig.

A: I think you are late.

        French: Je pense que tu es en retard.
        Spanish: Creo que llegas tarde.
        German: Ich glaube, du bist zu spät.

B: No. I am on time.

> French: Non, je suis à l'heure.
> Spanish: No. Llegué a tiempo.
> German: Nein, ich bin pünktlich.

A: Do you have a pen?

> French: Avez-vous un stylo?
> Spanish: ¿Tienes un bolígrafo?
> German: Hast du einen Stift?

B: Sorry. I do not have.

> French: Pardon. Je n'ai pas.
> Spanish: Lo siento. No tengo.
> German: Es tut uns leid. Ich habe nicht.

A: I will meet you tomorrow.

> French: Je te rencontrerai demain.
> Spanish: Mañana me reuniré contigo.
> German: Ich werde dich morgen treffen.

B: I will wait for you.

> French: Je vais vous attendre.
> Spanish: Te esperaré.
> German: Ich werde auf dich warten.

13. **Learn through Music**: Music and learning go hand in hand and can be an effective tool for learning a foreign language. Songs are a unique way of memorizing language concepts, pronunciation and structure. A learner is more likely to retain and memorize a language by singing a song rather than by just speaking the words or sentences as part of routine practice.

14. **Good Grammar**: It's no secret that grammar improves the development of fluency. When you learn the grammar structure of a language, organizing and expressing ideas in your mind will enable you to become a fluent and proficient speaker of the language.

Exercise
Do oral translation of these sentences in your learning language.

Excuse me.
Yes. Tell me.
Do you have a pen?
Sorry. I do not have.
I will meet you tomorrow.
I will wait for you.
I want to watch a movie.
Very good.

Lesson 5

It takes time to be fluent in a language you are learning. It may take probably months or years. However, with the right amount of commitment and focus on practicing more every day, you can be a fluent speaker in no time. Remember better fluency leads to greater understanding. Fluency in a foreign language is a major accomplishment. It's also a great way to increase your opportunities for employment and travel. Fluency is made up of several different factors, so it's important to work on each aspect: speaking, listening, reading, cultural literacy, and writing.

Food

A: What do you eat in breakfast?

    French: Que mangez-vous au petit-déjeuner?
    Spanish: ¿Qué comes en el desayuno?
    German: Was isst du beim Frühstück?

B: I eat apples.

    French: Je mange des pommes.
    Spanish: Yo como manzanas.
    German: Ich esse Äpfel.

A: Do you drink tea?

    French: Buvez-vous du thé?
    Spanish: ¿Tomas te?
    German: Trinkst du Tee?

B: I like coffee.

    French: J'aime le café.
    Spanish: Me gusta el café.
    German: Ich mag Kaffee.

A: Coffee of Europe is good.

    French: Le café d'Europe est bon.
    Spanish: El café de Europa es bueno.
    German: Kaffee von Europa ist gut.

B: Tea of India is also tasty.

    French: Le thé de l'Inde est également savoureux.
    Spanish: El té de la India también es sabroso.
    German: Tee aus Indien ist auch lecker.

A: What is the best food of India?

    French: Quelle est la meilleure nourriture de l'Inde?
    Spanish: ¿Cuál es la mejor comida de la India?
    German: Was ist das beste Essen von Indien?

B: We like rice and dal.
>French: Nous aimons le riz et le dal.
>Spanish: Nos gusta el arroz y el dal.
>German: Wir mögen Reis und Dal.

A: What is the best in your country?
>French: Quel est le meilleur dans votre pays?
>Spanish: ¿Qué es lo mejor de tu país?
>German: Was ist das Beste in Ihrem Land?

B: Cassoulet is the best food in France.
>French: Le cassoulet est la meilleure cuisine de France.
>Spanish: Cassoulet es la mejor comida de Francia.
>German: Cassoulet ist das beste Essen in Frankreich.

A: I am happy to meet you.
>French: Je suis heureux de vous rencontrer.
>Spanish: Estoy feliz de conocerte.
>German: Ich bin froh dich zu sehen.

B: Same here.
>French: Pareil ici.
>Spanish: La misma aquí.
>German: Hier gilt das gleiche.

How to make your language effective:
1. Listen to native speakers in natural contexts as much as possible. If you can't find live native speakers to eavesdrop on, watch movies and television shows in that language, or listen to books on tape or music in that language.

2. Practice speaking every day. Try to learn new words and phrases every day. It is also crucial to frequently practice the earlier words you have learned, in addition to newer words. If possible, practice with native speakers, and encourage them to correct you.

3. Record yourself speaking, then play it back and compare your inflection and pronunciation to that of native speakers.

Exercise
Do oral translation of these sentences in your learning language.

I greet you.
Good morning.
Do you drink tea?
I like coffee.
What is the best food of India?
We like rice and dal.
I am happy to meet you.

Lesson 6

French is a language of the Indo-European family. It descended from Latin of the Roman Empire, as did all Roman languages. French evolved from Gallo-Romance, the Latin spoken in Gaul, and more specifically in Northern Gaul. Its closest relatives are the other languages historically spoken in northern France and in southern Belgium, which French largely supplanted. French was also influenced by native Celtic languages of Northern Roman Gaul like Gallia Belgica and by the (Germanic) Frankish language of the post-Roman Frankish invaders. Today, owing to France's past overseas expansion, there are numerous French-based creole languages, most notably Haitian Creole. A French-speaking person or nation may be referred to as Francophone in both English and French.

French is an official language in 29 countries across multiple continents, most of which are members of the Organisation internationale de la Francophonie (OIF), the community of 84 countries which share the official use or teaching of French. French is also one of six official languages used in the United Nations. It is spoken as a first language in France; the Democratic Republic of Congo; Algeria; Morocco; Canada, Belgium, Ivory Coast; Tunisia; western Switzerland); Monaco; parts of Luxembourg; parts of the United States (the states of Louisiana, Maine, New Hampshire and Vermont); northwestern Italy; and various communities elsewhere.

Language

A: What is your first language?

    French: Quelle est votre langue maternelle?
    Spanish: ¿Cual es tu primer idioma?
    German: Was ist deine Muttersprache?

B: I speak English frequently.

    French: Je parle anglais fréquemment.
    Spanish: Hablo inglés con frecuencia.
    German: Ich spreche häufig Englisch.

A: What is your education?

    French: Quel est votre niveau d'etudes?
    Spanish: ¿Cuál es tu educación?
    German: Was hast du für eine Ausbildung?

B: I am a graduate.

    French: Je suis diplômé.
    Spanish: Soy graduada.
    German: Ich bin Absolvent.

A: Do you love literature?

    French: Vous aimez la littérature?
    Spanish: ¿Amas la literatura?
    German: Lieben Sie Literatur?

B: Yes. I read stories.
>> French: Oui. Je lis des histoires.
>> Spanish: Si. Leo cuentos.
>> German: Ja. Ich lese Geschichten.

A: Do you understand my language?
>> French: Comprenez-vous ma langue?
>> Spanish: ¿Entiendes mi idioma?
>> German: Verstehst du meine Sprache?

B: Yes. I like foreign languages.
>> French: Oui. J'aime les langues étrangères.
>> Spanish: Si. Me gustan los idiomas extranjeros.
>> German: Ja. Ich mag Fremdsprachen.

A: Which foreign language do you learn in school?
>> French: Quelle langue étrangère apprends-tu à l'école?
>> Spanish: ¿Qué idioma extranjero aprendes en la escuela?
>> German: Welche Fremdsprache lernt man in der Schule?

B: French was my first foreign language.
>> French: Le français a été ma première langue étrangère.
>> Spanish: El francés fue mi primera lengua extranjera.
>> German: Französisch war meine erste Fremdsprache.

Due to Roman rule, Latin was gradually adopted by the inhabitants of Gaul, and as the language was learned by the common people it developed a distinct local character, with grammatical differences from Latin as spoken elsewhere, some of which being attested on graffiti. This local variety evolved into the Gallo-Romance tongues, which include French and its closest relatives, such as Arpitan.

The evolution of Latin in Gaul was shaped by its coexistence for over half a millennium beside the native Celtic Gaulish language, which did not go extinct until the late 6th century, long after the Fall of the Western Roman Empire. The population remained 90% indigenous in origin; the Romanizing class was the local native elite whose children learned Latin in Roman schools. At the time of the collapse of the Empire, this local elite had been slowly abandoning Gaulish entirely, but the rural and lower class populations remained Gaulish speakers who could sometimes also speak Latin or Greek.

Exercise
Do oral translation of these sentences in your learning language.

What place is it?
It is a school.
Do you understand my language?
Yes. I like foreign languages.
What is your education?
I am a graduate.
Where do you live?

Lesson 7

The Gaulish language likely survived into the 6th century in France despite considerable Romanization. Coexisting with Latin, Gaulish helped shape the Latin dialects that developed into French. The French pronunciation changes shaped by Gaulish influence, and influences in conjugation and word order. The estimated number of French words that can be attributed to Gaulish is placed at 154 by the Petit Robert, which is often viewed as representing standardized French, while if non-standard dialects are included, the number increases to 240. Known Gaulish loans are skewed toward certain semantic fields.

Presentation

A: Who is the tall woman?

> French: Qui est la grande femme?
> Spanish: ¿Quién es la mujer alta?
> German: Wer ist die große Frau?

B: She is my friend.

> French: Elle est mon amie.
> Spanish: Ella es mi amiga.
> German: Sie ist meine Freundin.

A: Who is playing there?

> French: Qui joue là-bas?
> Spanish: ¿Quién juega ahí?
> German: Wer spielt da?

B: He is my relative.

> French: Il est mon parent.
> Spanish: El es mi pariente.
> German: Er ist mein Verwandter.

A: How many brothers do you have?

> French: Combien de frères as-tu?
> Spanish: ¿Cuántos hermanos tiene usted?
> German: Wie viele Brüder hast du?

B: I have two brothers.

> French: J'ai deux frères.
> Spanish: Tengo dos hermanos.
> German: Ich habe zwei Brüder.

A: What about your sisters?

> French: Et tes sœurs?
> Spanish: ¿Y tus hermanas?
> German: Was ist mit deinen Schwestern?

B: She is my sister.

        French: Elle est ma soeur.

        Spanish: Ella es mi hermana.

        German: Sie ist meine Schwester.

A: Where are your parents?

        French: Où sont tes parents?

        Spanish: ¿Dónde están tus padres?

        German: Wo sind deine Eltern?

B: They are with my uncle.

        French: Ils sont avec mon oncle.

        Spanish: Están con mi tío.

        German: Sie sind bei meinem Onkel.

A: What is their occupation?

        French: Quel est leur métier?

        Spanish: Cual es su ocupacion?

        German: Was ist ihr Beruf?

B: They are businessmen.

        French: Ce sont des hommes d'affaires.

        Spanish: Son hombres de negocios.

        German: Sie sind Geschäftsleute.

During the 17th century, French replaced Latin as the most important language of diplomacy and international relations. It retained this role until approximately the middle of the 20th century, when it was replaced by English as the United States became the dominant global power following the Second World War. During the Grand Siècle, France, under the rule of powerful leaders such as Cardinal Richelieu and Louis XIV, enjoyed a period of prosperity and prominence among European nations. Richelieu established the Académie française to protect the French language. By the early 1800s, Parisian French had become the primary language of the aristocracy in France.

Exercise

Do oral translation of these sentences in your learning language.

Do you drink tea?
I like coffee.
Where are your parents?
They are with my uncle.
What is their occupation?
They are businessmen.
Who is playing there?
He is my relative.
What is the best food of India?
We like rice and dal.

Lesson 8

Near the beginning of the 19th century, the French government began to pursue policies with the end goal of eradicating the many minorities and regional languages spoken in France. The goals of the Public School System were made especially clear to the French-speaking teachers sent to teach students in regions such as Occitania and Brittany. Instructions given by a French official to teachers in the department of Finistère, in western Brittany.

Spoken by 19.71% of the European Union's population, French is the third most widely spoken language in the EU, after English and German and the second most-widely taught language after English. Under the Constitution of France, French has been the official language of the Republic since 1992, although the ordinance of Villers-Cotterêts made it mandatory for legal documents in 1539. France mandates the use of French in official government publications, public education except in specific cases, and legal contracts; advertisements must bear a translation of foreign words.

In Belgium, French is an official language at the federal level along with Dutch and German. At the regional level, French is the sole official language of Wallonia and one of the two official languages—along with Dutch—of the Brussels-Capital Region, where it is spoken by the majority of the population. French is one of the four official languages of Switzerland, along with German, Italian, and Romansh, and is spoken in the western part of Switzerland, called Romandy, of which Geneva is the largest city. The language divisions in Switzerland do not coincide with political subdivisions, and some cantons have bilingual status: for example, cities such as Biel/Bienne and cantons such as Valais, Fribourg and Berne. French is the native language of about 23% of the Swiss population, and is spoken by 50% of the population.

General Questions

A: What is this?

    French: Qu'est-ce que c'est?
    Spanish: ¿Qué es ésto?
    German: Was ist das?

B: It is a book.

    French: C'est un livre.
    Spanish: Es un libro.
    German: Es ist ein Buch.

A: How old is it?

    French: Quel âge a-t-il?
    Spanish: ¿Qué edad tiene?
    German: Wie alt ist es?

B: It is new.

    French: C'est nouveau.
    Spanish: Es nuevo.
    German: Es ist neu.

A: How is the weather?
> French: Comment est la temps?
> Spanish: ¿Como está el clima?
> German: Wie ist das Wetter?

B: It is cold here.
> French: Il fait froid ici.
> Spanish: Hace frío aquí.
> German: Es ist kalt hier.

A: Which season do you like?
> French: Quelle saison aimez-vous?
> Spanish: ¿Qué temporada te gusta?
> German: Welche Jahreszeit magst du?

B: I like spring season.
> French: J'aime la saison printanière.
> Spanish: Me gusta la temporada de primavera.
> German: Ich mag die Frühlingssaison.

A: Is winter not good for you?
> French: L'hiver n'est-il pas bon pour vous?
> Spanish: ¿El invierno no es bueno para ti?
> German: Ist der Winter nicht gut für Sie?

B: Not at all.
> French: Pas du tout.
> Spanish: Para nada.
> German: Überhaupt nicht.

French is the second most common language in Canada, after English, and both are official languages at the federal level. It is the first language of 9.5 million people or 29% and the second language for 2.07 million or 6% of the entire population of Canada. French is the sole official language in the province of Quebec, being the mother tongue for some 7 million people, or almost 80% of the province. About 95% of the people of Quebec speak French as either their first or second language, and for some as their third language. Quebec is also home to the city of Montreal, which is the world's 4th-largest French-speaking city, by number of first language speakers.

Exercise
Do oral translation of these sentences in your learning language.

I am glad to see you.
It is my pleasure.
How is the weather?
It is cold here.
Which season do you like?
I like spring season.

Lesson 9

Spanish is a Roman language that originated in the Iberian Peninsula of Europe. Today, it is a global language with nearly 500 million native speakers, mainly in Spain and the Americas. It is the world's second-most spoken native language after Mandarin Chinese, and the world's fourth-most spoken language overall after English, Mandarin Chinese, and Hindi.

Spanish is a part of the Ibero-Romance group of languages of the Indo-European language family, which evolved from several dialects of Latin in Iberia after the collapse of the Western Roman Empire in the 5th century. The oldest Latin texts with traces of Spanish come from mid-northern Iberia in the 9th century, and the first systematic written use of the language happened in Toledo, a prominent city of the Kingdom of Castile, in the 13th century. Modern Spanish was then taken to the viceroyalties of the Spanish Empire beginning in 1492, most notably to the Americas, as well as territories in Africa and the Philippines.

As a Roman language, Spanish is a descendant of Latin and has one of the smaller degrees of difference from it (about 20%) alongside Sardinian and Italian. Around 75% of modern Spanish vocabulary is derived from Latin, including Latin borrowings from Ancient Greek. The abundance of Classical Greek words directly and indirectly incorporated in the Spanish language have notably influenced the vocabulary of elemental areas like nature, science, politics, literature, philosophy, arts, and music.

Restaurant

A: Where is a restaurant?

> French: Où est un restaurant?
> Spanish: ¿Dónde hay un restaurante?
> German: Wo gibt es ein Restaurant?

B: It is inside the mall.

> French: C'est à l'intérieur du centre commercial.
> Spanish: Está dentro del centro comercial.
> German: Es befindet sich im Einkaufszentrum.

A: How is the food here?

> French: Comment est la nourriture ici?
> Spanish: ¿Cómo está la comida aquí?
> German: Wie ist das Essen hier?

B: It is delicious.

> French: C'est délicieux.
> Spanish: Es delicioso.
> German: Es ist köstlich.

A: Is it expensive?

> French: Est-ce cher?
> Spanish: ¿Es caro?
> German: Ist es teuer?

B: No. It is cheap.

> French: Non, c'est bon marché.
> Spanish: No. Es barato.
> German: Nein, es ist billig.

A: Where can I pay?

> French: Où puis-je payer?
> Spanish: ¿Dónde puedo pagar?
> German: Wo kann ich bezahlen?

B: The counter is here.

> French: Le compteur est là.
> Spanish: El mostrador está aquí.
> German: Der Zähler ist da.

A: Please call the waiter.

> French: Veuillez appeler le serveur.
> Spanish: Por favor llame al camarero.
> German: Bitte rufen Sie den Kellner an.

B: Okay. He is coming.

> French: D'accord. Il arrive.
> Spanish: Bueno. Él viene.
> German: Okay. Er kommt.

Due to both its complex history and the formation of its global empire, the Spanish language has received some influences from many different languages: Additionally, it has absorbed vocabulary from other languages, particularly other Roman languages such as French, Italian, Portuguese, Galician, Catalan, Mozarabic, Occitan, and Sardinian, as well as from Quechua, Nahuatl, and other indigenous languages of the Americas. Spanish is one of the six official languages of the United Nations, and it is also used as an official language by the European Union, the Organization of American States, the Union of South American Nations, the Community of Latin American and Caribbean States, the African Union and many other international organizations. Spanish is the third most used language on internet websites after English and Russian.

Exercise
Do oral translation of these sentences in your learning language.

Do you understand my language?
Yes. I like foreign languages.
What is your education?
I am a graduate.
How is the food here?
It is delicious.
Is it expensive?
No. It is cheap.

Lesson 10

German language is mainly spoken in Central Europe. It is the most widely spoken and official or co-official language in Germany, Austria, Switzerland, Liechtenstein, and the Italian province of South Tyrol. It is also a co-official language of Luxembourg, Belgium and parts of southwestern Poland, as well as a national language in Namibia. German is most similar to other languages within the West Germanic language branch, including Afrikaans, Dutch, English, Frisian languages, Luxembourgish, Scots, and Yiddish. The pronunciation of German words are simple and similar to English.

One of the major languages of the world, German is a native language to almost 100 million people worldwide and is spoken by a total of over 130 million people. It is the most spoken native language within the European Union. German is also widely taught as a foreign language, especially in Europe, where it is the third most taught foreign language (after English and French), and the United States. The language has been influential in the fields of philosophy, theology, science and technology. It is the second most commonly used scientific language and among the most widely used languages on websites. The German-speaking countries are ranked fifth in terms of annual publication of new books, with one-tenth of all books (including e-books) in the world being published in German.

Interview

A: Please tell me your name.

French: S'il vous plait, dites moi votre nom.
Spanish: Porfavor dime tu nombre.
German: Verrate mir bitte deinen Namen.

B: My name is Niranjan Showman.

French: Je m'appelle Niranjan Showman.
Spanish: Mi nombre es Niranjan Showman.
German: Mein Name ist Niranjan Showman.

A: You can sit here.

French: Vous pouvez vous asseoir ici.
Spanish: Tu puedes sentarte aquí.
German: Du kannst hier sitzen.

B: Thank you so much.

French: Merci beaucoup.
Spanish: Muchas gracias.
German: Ich danke dir sehr.

A: Show me your document.

French: Montrez-moi votre document.
Spanish: Enséñame tu documento.
German: Zeigen Sie mir Ihr Dokument.

B: Give me a minute.

        French: Donne moi une minute.
        Spanish: Dame un minuto.
        German: Gib mir eine Minute.

A: What is your age?

        French: Quel âge avez-vous?
        Spanish: ¿Cuál es tu edad?
        German: Wie alt bist du?

B: I am thirty-five.

        French: J'ai trente-cinq ans.
        Spanish: Tengo treinta y cinco.
        German: Ich bin fünfunddreißig.

A: What is your ambition?

        French: Quelle est ton ambition?
        Spanish: ¿Cual es tu ambición?
        German: Was ist dein Beweggrund?

B: I want to be a scholar.

        French: Je veux être un érudit.
        Spanish: Quiero ser un erudito.
        German: Ich möchte Gelehrter werden.

If we talk as per grammar, German is an inflected language, with four cases for nouns, pronouns, and adjectives (nominative, accusative, genitive, dative); three genders (masculine, feminine, neuter); and two numbers (singular, plural). It has strong and weak verbs. The majority of its vocabulary derives from the ancient Germanic branch of the Indo-European language family, while a smaller share is partly derived from Latin and Greek, along with fewer words borrowed from French and Modern English. German is a polycentric language; the three standardized variants are German, Austrian, and Swiss Standard High German. It is also notable for its broad spectrum of dialects, with many varieties existing in Europe and other parts of the world. Some of these non-standard varieties have become recognized and protected by regional or national governments.

Exercise
Do oral translation of these sentences in your learning language.

Do you drink tea?
I like coffee.
You can sit here.
Thank you so much.
Show me your document.
Give me a minute.
What is your age?
I am thirty-five.

Lesson 11

Self-Introduction

My name is Niranjan Showman.
        French: Je m'appelle Niranjan Showman.
        Spanish: Mi nombre es Niranjan Showman.
        German: Mein Name ist Niranjan Showman.

I live in Mumbai, India.
        French: Je vis à Bombay, en Inde.
        Spanish: Vivo en Mumbai, India.
        German: Ich lebe in Mumbai, Indien.

My job is teaching languages.
        French: Mon travail est l'enseignement des langues.
        Spanish: Mi trabajo es enseñar idiomas.
        German: Meine Aufgabe ist es, Sprachen zu unterrichten.

I have written some books.
        French: J'ai écrit quelques livres.
        Spanish: He escrito algunos libros.
        German: Ich habe einige Bücher geschrieben.

I like to read books and watch movies.
        French: J'aime lire des livres et regarder des films.
        Spanish: Me gusta leer libros y ver películas.
        German: Ich mag Bücher lesen und Filme anschauen.

My city is beautiful and rich.
        French: Ma ville est belle et riche.
        Spanish: Mi ciudad es hermosa y rica.
        German: Meine Stadt ist schön und reich.

I have two brothers and no sister.
        French: J'ai deux frères et pas de soeur.
        Spanish: Tengo dos hermanos y ninguna hermana.
        German: Ich habe zwei Brüder und keine Schwester.

I am thirty-five years old.
        French: J'ai trente-cinq ans.
        Spanish: Tengo treinta y cinco años.
        German: Ich bin fünfunddreißig Jahre alt.

I can speak English and French.

    French: Je peux parler anglais et français.

    Spanish: Puedo hablar inglés y francés.

    German: Ich kann Englisch und Französisch sprechen.

My hobby is to visit new places.

    French: Mon hobby est de visiter de nouveaux endroits.

    Spanish: Mi afición es visitar nuevos lugares.

    German: Mein Hobby ist es, neue Orte zu besuchen.

Now I want to visit Europe.

    French: Maintenant, je veux visiter l'Europe.

    Spanish: Ahora quiero visitar Europa.

    German: Jetzt möchte ich Europa besuchen.

Speaking a foreign language is good for my career.

    French: Parler une langue étrangère est bon pour ma carrière.

    Spanish: Hablar un idioma extranjero es bueno para mi carrera.

    German: Eine Fremdsprache zu sprechen ist gut für meine Karriere.

Europeans are great discoverers.

    French: Les Européens sont de grands découvreurs.

    Spanish: Las europeas son grandes descubridoras.

    German: Europäer sind große Entdecker.

Thank you.

    French: Merci.

    Spanish: Gracias.

    German: Vielen Dank.

You need to deliver this speech in your classroom or among your friends and you should record your voice to gain confidence. When the primary goal for students is to practice speaking the target language, hear how they sound, and improve their speaking proficiency, being able to play back your own voice has proven to be very beneficial. This kind of self-monitoring is an important part for all levels of foreign language learners. Students are able to reflect on their accent, grammar, fluency, intonation, etc. Recording provides a variety of purposes, including self-assessment, group work, dialogues, links to culture, and teacher assessment.

On the other hand, when teaching children with foreign backgrounds whose native language is not the same language of the country they currently live in, recording voice can assist. It gives them time to put thoughts into words if they cannot read or write the language yet and when their speaking abilities are still limited. When learners record themselves speaking they can also be made aware of their pronunciation challenges and work towards eliminating them. Recording yourself can also create a safer space for new language learners than speaking out loud in front of a class.

Lesson 12

My City Mumbai

Mumbai is a big city of India.
>French: Mumbai est une grande ville de l'Inde.
>Spanish: Mumbai es una gran ciudad de la India.
>German: Mumbai ist eine große Stadt in Indien.

It is the financial capital of the country.
>French: C'est la capitale financière du pays.
>Spanish: Es la capital financiera del país.
>German: Es ist die Finanzhauptstadt des Landes.

I live in this city from twenty years.
>French: Je vis dans cette ville depuis vingt ans.
>Spanish: Vivo en esta ciudad desde hace veinte años.
>German: Ich lebe in dieser Stadt seit zwanzig Jahren.

Mumbai is thickly populated.
>French: Mumbai est densément peuplée.
>Spanish: Mumbai está densamente poblada.
>German: Mumbai ist dicht besiedelt.

People have very busy life here.
>French: Les gens ont une vie très occupée ici.
>Spanish: La gente tiene una vida muy ocupada aquí.
>German: Die Leute haben hier ein sehr beschäftigtes Leben.

Mumbai is famous for film production.
>French: Mumbai est célèbre pour la production cinématographique.
>Spanish: Mumbai es famosa por la producción de películas.
>German: Mumbai ist berühmt für seine Filmproduktion.

Many film stars live here.
>French: De nombreuses stars de cinéma vivent ici.
>Spanish: Aquí viven muchas estrellas de cine.
>German: Hier leben viele Filmstars.

Life is very expensive for all.
>French: La vie est très chère pour tous.
>Spanish: La vida es muy cara para todos.
>German: Das Leben ist für alle sehr teuer.

There are many beautiful places here.
> French: Il y a beaucoup de beaux endroits ici.
> Spanish: Hay muchos lugares hermosos aquí.
> German: Hier gibt es viele schöne Orte.

Local train is life-line of this city.
> French: Le train local est la ligne de vie de cette ville.
> Spanish: El tren local es la línea de vida de esta ciudad.
> German: Der Nahverkehrszug ist die Lebensader dieser Stadt.

I like this for its beauty.
> French: J'aime ça pour sa beauté.
> Spanish: Me gusta esto por su belleza.
> German: Ich mag das wegen seiner Schönheit.

I live here for prosperity.
> French: Je vis ici pour la prospérité.
> Spanish: Vivo aquí por la prosperidad.
> German: Ich lebe hier für Wohlstand.

Mumbai is a cosmopolitan cit.
> French: Mumbai est une ville cosmopolite.
> Spanish: Mumbai es una ciudad cosmopolita.
> German: Mumbai ist eine kosmopolitische Stadt.

I like this city for weather.
> French: J'aime cette ville pour le temps.
> Spanish: Me gusta esta ciudad por el clima.
> German: Ich mag diese Stadt wegen des Wetters.

Thank you.
> French: French: Merci.
> Spanish: Gracias.
> German: Vielen Dank.

One of the biggest hurdles to listening skill mastery can be our own perceptions. Poor mental frameworks can cause us to pursue time intensive but unrewarding tasks, give up quickly when we're faced with a challenge or simply not achieve as much as we would like to. When we're listening to anything, whether it be a conversation with a friend or a television drama, when we're starting out we should consider ourselves successful as long as we understand the gist of what we're listening to.

Another unfortunate belief that has stolen many an hour from language learners is that you can learn from passive listening. By passive listening I mean things like having the radio on in the background while you're focused on writing an essay or listening to music while trying to study for a brutal science test the next day. This kind of passive listening never helps you because there come many words and their pronunciation that you don't understand. We always suggest active listening.

Lesson 13

Our Country India

India is my country.
> French: L'Inde est mon pays.
> Spanish: India es mi país.
> German: Indien ist mein Land.

I am an Indian citizen.
> French: Je suis citoyen indien.
> Spanish: Soy ciudadana india.
> German: Ich bin indischer Staatsbürger.

Our country is in Asian continent.
> French: Notre pays est sur le continent asiatique.
> Spanish: Nuestro país está en el continente asiático.
> German: Unser Land liegt auf dem asiatischen Kontinent.

Our national language is Hindi.
> French: Notre langue nationale est l'hindi.
> Spanish: Nuestro idioma nacional es el hindi.
> German: Unsere Landessprache ist Hindi.

We have our national flag.
> French: Nous avons notre drapeau national.
> Spanish: Tenemos nuestra bandera nacional.
> German: Wir haben unsere Nationalflagge.

Hockey is our national sport.
> French: Le hockey est notre sport national.
> Spanish: El hockey es nuestro deporte nacional.
> German: Hockey ist unser Nationalsport.

Tiger is our national animal.
> French: Le tigre est notre animal national.
> Spanish: El tigre es nuestro animal nacional.
> German: Tiger ist unser Nationaltier.

There are many rivers in India.
> French: Il existe de nombreuses rivières en Inde.
> Spanish: Hay muchos ríos en la India.
> German: In Indien gibt es viele Flüsse.

This is the seventh largest country of the world.

> French: C'est le septième plus grand pays du monde.
> Spanish: Este es el séptimo país más grande del mundo.
> German: Dies ist das siebtgrößte Land der Welt.

India is a secular democratic country.

> French: L'Inde est un pays démocratique laïc.
> Spanish: India es un país democrático laico.
> German: Indien ist ein säkulares demokratisches Land.

We have New Delhi as capital.

> French: Nous avons New Delhi comme capitale.
> Spanish: Tenemos a Nueva Delhi como capital.
> German: Wir haben Neu-Delhi als Hauptstadt.

We believe in peace and prosperity.

> French: Nous croyons en la paix et la prospérité.
> Spanish: Nosotras creemos en la paz y la prosperidad.
> German: Wir glauben an Frieden und Wohlstand.

India is an agricultural region.

> French: L'Inde est une région agricole.
> Spanish: India es una región agrícola.
> German: Indien ist eine Agrarregion.

It has many beautiful places to visit.

> French: Il a beaucoup de beaux endroits à visiter.
> Spanish: Tiene muchos lugares hermosos para visitar.
> German: Es hat viele schöne Orte zu besuchen.

India has very nice weather.

> French: L'Inde a un temps très agréable.
> Spanish: India tiene un clima muy agradable.
> German: Indien hat sehr schönes Wetter.

I love my country.

> French: J'aime mon pays.
> Spanish: Amo mi país.
> German: Ich liebe mein Land.

Thank you.

> French: French: Merci.
> Spanish: Gracias.
> German: Vielen Dank.

Lesson 14

About France

France is a country in Europe.
> French: La France est un pays d'Europe.
> Spanish: Francia es un país de Europa.
> German: Frankreich ist ein Land in Europa.

Its neighbors are Germany, Italy and Belgium.
> French: Ses voisins sont l'Allemagne, l'Italie et la Belgique.
> Spanish: Sus vecinas son Alemania, Italia y Bélgica.
> German: Seine Nachbarn sind Deutschland, Italien und Belgien.

Paris is the capital of France.
> French: Paris est la capitale de la France.
> Spanish: París es la capital de Francia.
> German: Paris ist die Hauptstadt von Frankreich.

It is also a beautiful city.
> French: C'est aussi une belle ville.
> Spanish: También es una ciudad hermosa.
> German: Es ist auch eine schöne Stadt.

It is the most populated city of the country.
> French: C'est la ville la plus peuplée du pays.
> Spanish: Es la ciudad más poblada del país.
> German: Es ist die bevölkerungsreichste Stadt des Landes.

French is the national language of France.
> French: Le français est la langue nationale de la France.
> Spanish: El francés es el idioma nacional de Francia.
> German: Französisch ist die Nationalsprache Frankreichs.

This country has eighteen regions.
> French: Ce pays compte dix-huit régions.
> Spanish: Este país tiene dieciocho regiones.
> German: Dieses Land hat achtzehn Regionen.

The total population is sixty-seven million.
> French: La population totale est de soixante-sept millions.
> Spanish: La población total es de sesenta y siete millones.
> German: Die Gesamtbevölkerung beträgt siebenundsechzig Millionen.

Marseille is the second largest city.
> French: Marseille est la deuxième plus grande ville.
> Spanish: Marsella es la segunda ciudad más grande.
> German: Marseille ist die zweitgrößte Stadt.

It has the biggest port in France.
> French: Elle possède le plus grand port de France.
> Spanish: Tiene el puerto más grande de Francia.
> German: Es hat den größten Hafen in Frankreich.

French culture is more than two thousand year old.
> French: La culture française a plus de deux mille ans.
> Spanish: La cultura francesa tiene más de dos mil años.
> German: Die französische Kultur ist mehr als zweitausend Jahre alt.

French cooking is superb to mankind.
> French: La cuisine française est superbe pour l'humanité.
> Spanish: La cocina francesa es excelente para la humanidad.
> German: Die französische Küche ist großartig für die Menschheit.

Thank you.
> French: French: Merci.
> Spanish: Gracias.
> German: Vielen Dank.

After learning French, the opportunities are going to be within French-speaking countries like France, Quebec in Canada, French parts of Switzerland and Belgium, or with companies originating from there that would like their employees to be able to communicate effectively. Remember that these companies want you to be fluent in French, so if you start learning today, it takes a year to become fluent in French language going through Basic, then A1, and then A2 level by passing exams of French Education Ministry. In terms of level, you would need at least A2 level on the European language scale. Because, if wish to really communicate well, A2 level would be better.

French faculties are paid high because of the increasing number of foreign language learners in India. Even the students of high schools are also having French as the academic subject in India. In India, French is the only foreign language that has more clubs and facilities. If you are interested in working abroad and you need to pass TOEFL for English. In France, you are allowed to enter only by passing at least grade A1 in French and DELF entrance exam is also compulsory. If you have finished production engineering, many French firms are very keen on employing people with more technical and practical. But entering France is not easy, if it happened, it is with all about your passion and love towards French language.

You can speaking French after doing just Basic course also, but there are many opportunities after learning French up to A2 level. Once you have passed the exam of A2 level, you can work for an embassy, you can be a teacher, or you can apply for United Nations as an interpreter. You can also be a tourist guide, work for hotels, or simply immigrate to France and live permanently. And you, being an engineer can get the most out of it by earning more than your expectation.

Lesson 15

About Spain

Spain is a country in Europe.
> French: L'Espagne est un pays d'Europe.
> Spanish: España es un país de Europa.
> German: Spanien ist ein Land in Europa.

Its neighbors are Portugal and France.
> French: Ses voisins sont le Portugal et la France.
> Spanish: Sus vecinas son Portugal y Francia.
> German: Seine Nachbarn sind Portugal und Frankreich.

Madrid is the capital of Spain.
> French: Madrid est la capitale de l'Espagne.
> Spanish: Madrid es la capital de España.
> German: Madrid ist die Hauptstadt von Spanien.

Madrid is also a beautiful city.
> French: Madrid est aussi une belle ville.
> Spanish: Madrid también es una ciudad preciosa.
> German: Madrid ist auch eine schöne Stadt.

Spanish is the national language of Spain.
> French: L'espagnol est la langue nationale de l'Espagne.
> Spanish: El español es el idioma nacional de España.
> German: Spanisch ist die Landessprache Spaniens.

Spain has fifty provinces.
> French: L'Espagne compte cinquante provinces.
> Spanish: España tiene cincuenta provincias.
> German: Spanien hat fünfzig Provinzen.

It has forty-seven million population.
> French: Il a quarante-sept millions d'habitants.
> Spanish: Tiene cuarenta y siete millones de habitantes.
> German: Es hat siebenundvierzig Millionen Einwohner.

Barcelona is the second largest city.
> French: Barcelone est la deuxième plus grande ville.
> Spanish: Barcelona es la segunda ciudad más grande.
> German: Barcelona ist die zweitgrößte Stadt.

This is famous for architecture.

      French: Ceci est célèbre pour l'architecture.
      Spanish: Esto es famoso por la arquitectura.
      German: Dies ist berühmt für die Architektur.

Spain is famous for football.

      French: L'Espagne est célèbre pour le football.
      Spanish: España es famosa por el fútbol.
      German: Spanien ist berühmt für Fußball.

Festival San Fermin has global attraction.

      French: Festival San Fermin a une attraction mondiale.
      Spanish: Festival San Fermín tiene atracción global.
      German: Festival San Fermin hat weltweite Anziehungskraft.

They play with tomatoes in La Tomatina.

      French: Ils jouent avec des tomates à La Tomatina.
      Spanish: Ellos juegan con tomates en La Tomatina.
      German: In La Tomatina spielen sie mit Tomaten.

Thank you.

      French: French: Merci.
      Spanish: Gracias.
      German: Vielen Dank.

Many people are surprised to find out that Spanish has more native speakers than English does, making it the second most spoken language in the world after Mandarin. As the pronunciation of this language is easy, compared to other European language, people tend to speak Spanish easily. The developing countries in Latin America are giving job opportunities to people fluent in Spanish. Spanish is indeed one of the best languages to learn if you want great employment options. You can easily get the job of an interpreter or translator in an MNC. The best part is that these jobs come with great salary packages even for fresher. There are ample of other job options in teaching, IT industry, export-import houses, pharmaceutical sector and financial institutes.

Spanish is now taught in almost every other school so you can easily get the job of a teacher. It is also the part of curriculum in various colleges. Also, a number of companies are looking forward to expand their business in Spain. Thus, they highly prefer candidates adept in Spanish these days. They get an upper hand as compared to other candidates. It really helps people securing jobs in BPO industry because from a part of Europe and almost entire Latin America, when people call to customer care, they want their call to be answered in Spanish.

People working in cruise line prefer Spanish as a survival language because Spanish people have more influence in this field. Spanish is also similar (not much) to Italian and Greek, so people of Italy and Greek find Spanish as common language to talk. As many words of Spanish are directly adopted from Greek and Italian. Almost all of my students who are learning Spanish from me, belong to cruise line and they find Spanish good for their long career.

Lesson 16

About Germany

Germany is a country in Europe.
>French: L'Allemagne est un pays d'Europe.
>Spanish: Alemania es un país en Europa.
>German: Deutschland ist ein Land in Europa.

Its neighbors are Austria, Switzerland and France.
>French: Ses voisins sont l'Autriche, la Suisse et la France.
>Spanish: Sus vecinos son Austria, Suiza y Francia.
>German: Seine Nachbarn sind Österreich, die Schweiz und Frankreich.

Berlin is the capital of Germany.
>French: Berlin est la capitale de l'Allemagne.
>Spanish: Berlín es la capital de Alemania.
>German: Berlin ist die Hauptstadt von Deutschland.

It is a beautiful city.
>French: C'est une belle ville.
>Spanish: Es una hermosa ciudad.
>German: Es ist eine schöne Stadt.

It is also the largest city of Germany.
>French: C'est aussi la plus grande ville d'Allemagne.
>Spanish: También es la ciudad más grande de Alemania.
>German: Sie ist auch die größte Stadt Deutschlands.

German is the national language of Germany.
>French: L'allemand est la langue nationale de l'Allemagne.
>Spanish: El alemán es el idioma nacional de Alemania.
>German: Deutsch ist die Landessprache Deutschlands.

This country has sixteen states.
>French: Ce pays compte seize états.
>Spanish: Este país tiene dieciséis estados.
>German: Dieses Land hat sechzehn Staaten.

Germany has eighty-three million population.
>French: L'Allemagne a quatre-vingt-trois millions d'habitants.
>Spanish: Alemania tiene ochenta y tres millones de habitantes.
>German: Deutschland hat dreiundachtzig Millionen Einwohner.

Frankfurt is the financial capital.
> French: Francfort est la capitale financière.
> Spanish: Frankfurt es la capital financiera.
> German: Frankfurt ist die Finanzhauptstadt.

This city has the busiest airport.
> French: Cette ville a l'aéroport le plus achalandé.
> Spanish: Esta ciudad tiene el aeropuerto más transitado.
> German: Diese Stadt hat den verkehrsreichsten Flughafen.

Ruhrgebiet is biggest urban area.
> French: Ruhrgebiet est la plus grande zone urbaine.
> Spanish: Ruhrgebiet es el área urbana más grande.
> German: Das Ruhrgebiet ist das größte Stadtgebiet.

Volkswagen is a German car manufacturer.
> French: Volkswagen est un constructeur automobile allemand.
> Spanish: Volkswagen es un fabricante de automóviles alemán.
> German: Volkswagen ist ein deutscher Autohersteller.

Germania was the old name of Germany.
> French: Germania était l'ancien nom de l'Allemagne.
> Spanish: Germania era el antiguo nombre de Alemania.
> German: Germania war der alte Name Deutschlands.

Now it is a great power with strong economy.
> French: Maintenant, c'est une grande puissance avec une économie forte.
> Spanish: Ahora es una gran potencia con una economía fuerte.
> German: Jetzt ist es eine Großmacht mit starker Wirtschaft.

Thank you.
> French: French: Merci.
> Spanish: Gracias.
> German: Vielen Dank.

Learning a foreign language is very good. There is a growing demand in the market for students with a working knowledge of German. With MNCs setting up operations in the region, the requirement for professionals with knowledge of foreign languages is increasing. Germany is home to numerous international corporations like Daimler Chrysier, Siemens, Bosch and SAP. German companies are among the world's largest exporters. You can explore jobs in corporate world that look for people who know and understand their language. If you hold any other degree apart from the diploma in German language, you may look out for job opportunities with German companies in that field. You could explore job opportunities as Engineers, Doctors, Advertising Copywriter, Advertising Manager, Art Dealer, Bilingual Educator, Court Interpreter, Editor, Fashion Buyer, Foreign Service Officer, International Hotel Administrator, International Consultant, Interpreter, Journalist, Multi-Lingual Port Receptionist, Overseas Personnel Manager, Pharmaceutical Representative, Professor, Proofreader, Publishing Specialist, Reporter, Scientific Linguist, Scientific Interpreter, TESO/ESL Teacher, Travel Agent Tour Organizer etc.

Lesson 17

Story Speaking

The Boy Who Cried Wolf (English)

In a village, lived a carefree boy with his father. The boy's father told him that he was old enough to watch over the sheep while they graze in the fields. Every day, he had to take the sheep to the grassy fields and watch them as they graze. However, the boy was unhappy and didn't want to take the sheep to the fields. He wanted to run and play, not watch the boring sheep graze in the field. So, he decided to have some fun. He cried, "Wolf! Wolf!" until the entire village came running with stones to chase away the wolf before it could eat any of the sheep. When the villagers saw that there was no wolf, they left muttering under their breath about how the boy had wasted their time. The next day, the boy cried once more, "Wolf! Wolf!" and, again, the villagers rushed there to chase the wolf away.

The boy laughed at the fright he had caused. This time, the villagers left angrily. The third day, as the boy went up the small hill, he suddenly saw a wolf attacking his sheep. He cried as hard as he could, "Wolf! Wolf! Wolf!", but not a single villager came to help him. The villagers thought that he was trying to fool them again and did not come to rescue him or his sheep. The little boy lost many sheep that day, all because of his foolishness.

The Boy Who Cried Wolf (French)
Le garçon qui criait au loup

Dans un village, vivait un garçon insouciant avec son père. Le père du garçon lui a dit qu'il était assez vieux pour surveiller les moutons pendant qu'ils paissent dans les champs. Chaque jour, il devait emmener les moutons dans les champs herbeux et les regarder paître. Cependant, le garçon était mécontent et ne voulait pas emmener les moutons dans les champs. Il voulait courir et jouer, pas regarder les moutons ennuyeux paître dans le champ. Alors, il a décidé de s'amuser. Il cria : « Loup ! Loup!" jusqu'à ce que tout le village accourut avec des pierres pour chasser le loup avant qu'il ne puisse manger aucun des moutons. Quand les villageois ont vu qu'il n'y avait pas de loup, ils sont partis en marmonnant sur la façon dont le garçon avait perdu leur temps. Le lendemain, le garçon cria une fois de plus : « Loup ! Loup!" et, encore une fois, les villageois s'y sont précipités pour chasser le loup.

Le garçon se mit à rire de l'effroi qu'il avait causé. Cette fois, les villageois sont partis en colère. Le troisième jour, alors que le garçon gravissait la petite colline, il vit soudain un loup attaquer ses moutons. Il cria aussi fort qu'il le put : « Loup ! Loup! Loup ! », mais pas un seul villageois n'est venu l'aider. Les villageois pensaient qu'il essayait à nouveau de les tromper et ne sont pas venus le sauver, lui ou ses moutons. Le petit garçon a perdu beaucoup de moutons ce jour-là, tout cela à cause de sa folie.

The Boy Who Cried Wolf (Spanish)
El niño que lloró lobo

En un pueblo, vivía un niño despreocupado con su padre. El padre del niño le dijo que tenía la edad suficiente para cuidar de las ovejas mientras pastan en los campos. Todos los días, tenía que llevar a las ovejas a los campos de hierba y observarlas mientras pastaban. Sin embargo, el niño no estaba contento y no quería llevarse las ovejas al campo. Quería correr y jugar, no ver a las aburridas ovejas pastar en el campo. Entonces, decidió divertirse. Gritó: "¡Lobo! ¡Lobo!" hasta que todo el pueblo llegó corriendo con piedras para ahuyentar al lobo antes de que pudiera comerse a las ovejas. Cuando los aldeanos vieron que no había ningún lobo, se fueron murmurando en voz baja sobre cómo el chico había perdido el tiempo. Al día siguiente, el niño gritó una vez más: "¡Lobo! ¡Lobo!" y, de nuevo, los aldeanos se apresuraron a ahuyentar al lobo.

El niño se rió del susto que había causado. Esta vez, los aldeanos se fueron enojados. El tercer día, cuando el niño subía la pequeña colina, de repente vio a un lobo atacando a sus ovejas. Lloró tan fuerte como pudo, "¡Lobo! ¡Lobo! ¡Lobo!", Pero ni un solo aldeano vino a ayudarlo. Los aldeanos pensaron que estaba tratando de engañarlos nuevamente y no vinieron a rescatarlo ni a él ni a sus ovejas. El niño perdió muchas ovejas ese día, todo a causa de su necedad.

The Boy Who Cried Wolf (German)
Der Junge, der "Wolf" schrie

In einem Dorf lebte ein unbeschwerter Junge mit seinem Vater. Der Vater des Jungen sagte ihm, dass er alt genug sei, um über die Schafe zu wachen, während sie auf den Feldern grasen. Jeden Tag musste er die Schafe auf die Wiesen bringen und ihnen beim Grasen zusehen. Der Junge war jedoch unglücklich und wollte die Schafe nicht auf die Felder bringen. Er wollte laufen und spielen, nicht den langweiligen Schafen beim Grasen zusehen. Also beschloss er, etwas Spaß zu haben. Er rief: „Wolf! Wolf!" bis das ganze Dorf mit Steinen angerannt kam, um den Wolf zu verjagen, bevor er eines der Schafe fressen konnte. Als die Dorfbewohner sahen, dass es keinen Wolf gab, gingen sie leise vor sich hin und murmelten, wie der Junge ihre Zeit verschwendet hatte. Am nächsten Tag rief der Junge noch einmal: „Wolf! Wolf!" und wieder eilten die Dorfbewohner dorthin, um den Wolf zu verjagen.

Der Junge lachte über den Schrecken, den er verursacht hatte. Diesmal gingen die Dorfbewohner wütend. Am dritten Tag, als der Junge den kleinen Hügel hinaufstieg, sah er plötzlich, wie ein Wolf seine Schafe angriff. Er schrie so laut er konnte: „Wolf! Wolf! Wolf!", aber kein einziger Dorfbewohner kam, um ihm zu helfen. Die Dorfbewohner dachten, dass er sie wieder täuschen wollte und kamen nicht, um ihn oder seine Schafe zu retten. Der kleine Junge verlor an diesem Tag viele Schafe, alles wegen seiner Dummheit.

Lesson 18

Story Speaking

The Lion and the Mouse (English)

A lion was once sleeping in the jungle when a mouse started running up and down his body just for fun. This disturbed the lion's sleep, and he woke up quite angry. He was about to eat the mouse when the mouse desperately requested the lion to set him free. "I promise you, I will be of great help to you someday if you save me." The lion laughed at the mouse's confidence and let him go.

One day, a few hunters came into the forest and took the lion with them. They tied him up against a tree. The lion was struggling to get out and started to whimper. Soon, the mouse walked past and noticed the lion in trouble. Quickly, he ran and gnawed on the ropes to set the lion free. Both of them sped off into the jungle.

The Lion and the Mouse (French)
Le lion et la souris

Un lion dormait autrefois dans la jungle quand une souris a commencé à courir le long de son corps juste pour s'amuser. Cela a perturbé le sommeil du lion, et il s'est réveillé assez en colère. Il était sur le point de manger la souris quand la souris a désespérément demandé au lion de le libérer. "Je vous promets que je vous serai d'une grande aide un jour si vous me sauvez." Le lion se mit à rire de la confiance de la souris et le laissa partir.

Un jour, quelques chasseurs sont entrés dans la forêt et ont emmené le lion avec eux. Ils l'ont attaché contre un arbre. Le lion avait du mal à sortir et se mit à gémir. Bientôt, la souris passa devant et remarqua le lion en difficulté. Rapidement, il a couru et a rongé les cordes pour libérer le lion. Tous deux s'enfuirent dans la jungle.

The Lion and the Mouse (Spanish)
El león y el ratón

Una vez, un león dormía en la jungla cuando un ratón comenzó a correr arriba y abajo por su cuerpo solo por diversión. Esto perturbó el sueño del león y se despertó bastante enojado. Estaba a punto de comerse al ratón cuando el ratón le pidió desesperadamente al león que lo dejara libre. "Te prometo que algún día te seré de gran ayuda si me salvas". El león se rió de la confianza del ratón y lo dejó ir.

Un día, algunos cazadores llegaron al bosque y se llevaron al león con ellos. Lo ataron contra un árbol. El león estaba luchando por salir y empezó a gimotear. Pronto, el ratón pasó y notó que el león estaba en problemas. Rápidamente, corrió y mordió las cuerdas para liberar al león. Ambos se adentraron en la jungla.

The Lion and the Mouse (German)
Der Löwe und die Maus

Ein Löwe schlief einst im Dschungel, als eine Maus aus Spaß an seinem Körper auf und ab lief. Dies störte den Schlaf des Löwen und er wachte ziemlich wütend auf. Er wollte gerade die Maus essen, als die Maus den Löwen verzweifelt bat, ihn freizulassen. „Ich verspreche dir, ich werde dir eines Tages eine große Hilfe sein, wenn du mich rettest." Der Löwe lachte über das Vertrauen der Maus und ließ ihn gehen.

Eines Tages kamen ein paar Jäger in den Wald und nahmen den Löwen mit. Sie fesselten ihn an einen Baum. Der Löwe kämpfte um herauszukommen und begann zu wimmern. Bald ging die Maus vorbei und bemerkte den Löwen in Schwierigkeiten. Schnell rannte er und nagte an den Seilen, um den Löwen zu befreien. Beide rasten in den Dschungel.

Lesson 19

Story Speaking

The Fox and the Stork (English)

One day, a selfish fox invited a stork for dinner. Stork was very happy with the invitation – she reached the fox's home on time and knocked at the door with her long beak. The fox took her to the dinner table and served some soup in shallow bowls for both of them.

As the bowl was too shallow for the stork, she couldn't have soup at all. But, the fox licked up his soup quickly. The stork was angry and upset, but she didn't show her anger and behaved politely. To teach a lesson to the fox, she then invited him for dinner the next day. She too served soup, but this time the soup was served in two tall narrow vases. The stork devoured the soup from her vase, but the fox couldn't drink any of it because of his narrow neck. The fox realised his mistake and went home famished.

The Fox and the Stork (French)
Le renard et la cigogne

Un jour, un renard égoïste a invité une cigogne à dîner. Stork était très contente de l'invitation - elle a atteint la maison du renard à temps et a frappé à la porte avec son long bec. Le renard l'a emmenée à table et leur a servi de la soupe dans des bols peu profonds.

Comme le bol était trop peu profond pour la cigogne, elle ne pouvait pas du tout manger de soupe. Mais, le renard a léché sa soupe rapidement. La cigogne était en colère et bouleversée, mais elle n'a pas montré sa colère et s'est comportée poliment. Pour donner une leçon au renard, elle l'invita alors à dîner le lendemain. Elle aussi servait de la soupe, mais cette fois la soupe était servie dans deux grands vases étroits. La cigogne a dévoré la soupe de son vase, mais le renard n'a pas pu en boire à cause de son cou étroit. Le renard réalisa son erreur et rentra chez lui affamé.

The Fox and the Stork (Spanish)
El zorro y la cigüeña

Un día, un zorro egoísta invitó a una cigüeña a cenar. Stork estaba muy contenta con la invitación: llegó a la casa del zorro a tiempo y llamó a la puerta con su largo pico. El zorro la llevó a la mesa del comedor y sirvió un poco de sopa en platos hondos para ambos.

Como el cuenco era demasiado poco profundo para la cigüeña, no podía comer sopa en absoluto. Pero, el zorro lamió su sopa rápidamente. La cigüeña estaba enojada y molesta, pero no mostró su enojo y se comportó cortésmente. Para darle una lección al zorro, ella lo invitó a cenar al día siguiente. Ella también sirvió sopa, pero esta vez la sopa se sirvió en dos jarrones altos y estrechos. La cigüeña devoró la sopa de su jarrón, pero el zorro no pudo beber nada debido a su cuello estrecho. El zorro se dio cuenta de su error y se fue a casa hambriento.

The Fox and the Stork (German)
Der Fuchs und der Storch

Eines Tages lud ein selbstsüchtiger Fuchs einen Storch zum Essen ein. Stork freute sich sehr über die Einladung – sie erreichte pünktlich das Haus des Fuchses und klopfte mit ihrem langen Schnabel an die Tür. Der Fuchs führte sie zum Esstisch und servierte beiden etwas Suppe in flachen Schüsseln.

Da die Schüssel für den Storch zu flach war, konnte sie überhaupt keine Suppe essen. Aber der Fuchs leckte seine Suppe schnell auf. Der Storch war wütend und aufgebracht, aber sie zeigte ihre Wut nicht und benahm sich höflich. Um dem Fuchs eine Lektion zu erteilen, lud sie ihn am nächsten Tag zum Abendessen ein. Auch sie servierte Suppe, aber diesmal wurde die Suppe in zwei hohen, schmalen Vasen serviert. Der Storch verschlang die Suppe aus ihrer Vase, aber der Fuchs konnte wegen seines schmalen Halses nichts davon trinken. Der Fuchs erkannte seinen Fehler und ging ausgehungert nach Hause.

Lesson 20

Story Speaking

The Golden Touch (English)

Once there lived a greedy man in a small town. He was very rich, and he loved gold and all things fancy. But he loved his daughter more than anything. One day, he chanced upon a fairy. The fairy's hair was caught in a few tree branches. He helped her out, but as his greediness took over, he realised that he had an opportunity to become richer by asking for a wish in return (by helping her out).

The fairy granted him a wish. He said, "All that I touch should turn to gold." And his wish was granted by the grateful fairy. The greedy man rushed home to tell his wife and daughter about his wish, all the while touching stones and pebbles and watching them convert into gold. Once he got home, his daughter rushed to greet him. As soon as he bent down to scoop her up in his arms, she turned into a gold statue. He was devastated and started crying and trying to bring his daughter back to life. He realised his folly and spent the rest of his days searching for the fairy to take away his wish.

The Golden Touch (French)
Le toucher d'or

Il était une fois un homme cupide dans une petite ville. Il était très riche, et il aimait l'or et toutes les choses de fantaisie. Mais il aimait sa fille plus que tout. Un jour, il tombe sur une fée. Les cheveux de la fée étaient pris dans quelques branches d'arbres. Il l'a aidée, mais alors que sa cupidité prenait le dessus, il s'est rendu compte qu'il avait l'opportunité de s'enrichir en lui demandant un vœu en retour (en l'aidant).

La fée lui exauça un vœu. Il a dit : « Tout ce que je touche doit se transformer en or. » Et son vœu fut exaucé par la fée reconnaissante. L'homme avide s'est précipité chez lui pour faire part de son souhait à sa femme et à sa fille, tout en touchant des pierres et des cailloux et en les regardant se transformer en or. Une fois rentré chez lui, sa fille s'est précipitée pour le saluer. Dès qu'il se pencha pour la prendre dans ses bras, elle se transforma en une statue en or. Il était dévasté et a commencé à pleurer et à essayer de ramener sa fille à la vie. Il réalisa sa folie et passa le reste de ses jours à chercher la fée pour emporter son souhait.

The Golden Touch (Spanish)
El toque dorado

Una vez vivía un hombre codicioso en una pequeña ciudad. Era muy rico y amaba el oro y todas las cosas lujosas. Pero amaba a su hija más que a nada. Un día, se encontró con un hada. El cabello del hada quedó atrapado en algunas ramas de árbol. Él la ayudó, pero cuando su codicia se hizo cargo, se dio cuenta de que tenía la oportunidad de enriquecerse pidiendo un deseo a cambio (ayudándola).

El hada le concedió un deseo. Dijo: "Todo lo que toco debe convertirse en oro". Y su deseo fue concedido por el hada agradecida. El hombre codicioso corrió a casa para contarle a su esposa e hija sobre su deseo, mientras tocaba piedras y guijarros y los veía convertirse en oro. Una vez que llegó a casa, su hija se apresuró a saludarlo. Tan pronto como se inclinó para levantarla en sus brazos, ella se convirtió en una estatua de oro. Estaba devastado y comenzó a llorar y a tratar de revivir a su hija. Se dio cuenta de su locura y pasó el resto de sus días buscando al hada que le quitara el deseo.

The Golden Touch (German)
Die goldene Note
Es lebte einmal ein gieriger Mann in einer kleinen Stadt. Er war sehr reich, und er liebte Gold und alles Schöne. Aber er liebte seine Tochter über alles. Eines Tages traf er zufällig auf eine Fee. Die Haare der Fee waren in ein paar Ästen gefangen. Er half ihr aus, aber als seine Gier überhand nahm, erkannte er, dass er die Möglichkeit hatte, reicher zu werden, indem er um einen Wunsch im Gegenzug bat (indem er ihr half).

Die Fee erfüllte ihm einen Wunsch. Er sagte: "Alles, was ich berühre, sollte zu Gold werden." Und sein Wunsch wurde von der dankbaren Fee erfüllt. Der gierige Mann eilte nach Hause, um seiner Frau und seiner Tochter von seinem Wunsch zu erzählen, während er Steine und Kieselsteine berührte und zusah, wie sie sich in Gold verwandelten. Als er nach Hause kam, beeilte sich seine Tochter, ihn zu begrüßen. Sobald er sich bückte, um sie in seine Arme zu nehmen, verwandelte sie sich in eine goldene Statue. Er war am Boden zerstört und fing an zu weinen und versuchte, seine Tochter wieder zum Leben zu erwecken. Er erkannte seine Torheit und verbrachte den Rest seines Tages damit, nach der Fee zu suchen, die ihm seinen Wunsch nahm.

Lesson 21

Story Speaking

The Greedy Lion (English)

On a hot day, a lion in the forest started feeling hungry. He was starting to hunt for his food when he found a hare roaming around alone. Instead of catching the hare, the lion let it go – "A small hare such as this can't satisfy my hunger", he said and scoffed. Then, a beautiful deer passed by and he decided to take his chances – he ran and ran behind the deer but since he was weak because of the hunger, he struggled to keep up with the deer's speed. Tired and defeated, the lion went back to look for the hare to fill up his stomach for the time being, but it was gone. The lion was sad and remained hungry for a long time.

The Greedy Lion (French)
Le lion gourmand

Par une chaude journée, un lion dans la forêt a commencé à avoir faim. Il commençait à chasser pour sa nourriture quand il a trouvé un lièvre errant seul. Au lieu d'attraper le lièvre, le lion l'a lâché - "Un petit lièvre comme celui-ci ne peut pas satisfaire ma faim", a-t-il dit en se moquant. Puis, un beau cerf est passé et il a décidé de tenter sa chance - il a couru et couru derrière le cerf mais comme il était faible à cause de la faim, il a eu du mal à suivre la vitesse du cerf. Fatigué et vaincu, le lion est retourné chercher le lièvre pour remplir son estomac pour le moment, mais il était parti. Le lion était triste et resta affamé longtemps.

The Greedy Lion (Spanish)
El león codicioso

En un día caluroso, un león en el bosque comenzó a sentir hambre. Estaba empezando a buscar su comida cuando se encontró con una liebre deambulando sola. En lugar de atrapar a la liebre, el león la soltó: "Una liebre pequeña como esta no puede satisfacer mi hambre", dijo y se burló. Entonces, pasó un hermoso ciervo y decidió arriesgarse: corrió y corrió detrás del ciervo, pero como estaba débil debido al hambre, luchó por mantener la velocidad del ciervo. Cansado y derrotado, el león volvió a buscar la liebre para llenar su estómago por el momento, pero ya no estaba. El león estaba triste y permaneció hambriento durante mucho tiempo.

The Greedy Lion (German)
Der gierige Löwe

An einem heißen Tag bekam ein Löwe im Wald Hunger. Er fing an, nach seinem Essen zu suchen, als er einen allein umherstreifenden Hasen fand. Anstatt den Hasen zu fangen, ließ der Löwe ihn los – „Ein kleiner Hase wie dieser kann meinen Hunger nicht stillen", sagte er und spottete. Dann kam ein wunderschönes Reh vorbei und er beschloss, sein Risiko einzugehen – er rannte und rannte hinter dem Reh her, aber da er vor Hunger schwach war, hatte er Mühe, mit der Geschwindigkeit des Rehs Schritt zu halten. Müde und geschlagen ging der Löwe zurück, um den Hasen zu suchen, um sich vorerst den Magen zu füllen, aber er war weg. Der Löwe war traurig und blieb lange hungrig.

Lesson 22

Story Speaking

The Milkmaid and Her Pail (English)

Patty, a milkmaid milked her cow and had two full pails of fresh, creamy milk. She put both pails of milk on a stick and set off to the market to sell the milk. As she took steps towards the market, her thoughts took steps towards wealth. On her way, she kept thinking about the money she would make from selling the milk. Then she thought about what she would do with that money.

She was talking to herself and said, "Once I get the money, I'll buy a chicken. The chicken will lay eggs and I will get more chickens. They'll all lay eggs, and I will sell them for more money. Then, I'll buy the house on the hill and everyone will envy me." She was very happy that soon she would be very rich. With these happy thoughts, she marched ahead. But suddenly, she tripped and fell. Both the pails of the milk fell and all her dreams were shattered. The milk spilt onto the ground, and all Patty could do was cry. "No more dream," she cried foolishly!

The Milkmaid and Her Pail (French)
La laitière et son seau

Patty, une laitière traitait sa vache et avait deux seaux pleins de lait frais et crémeux. Elle mit les deux seaux de lait sur un bâton et partit au marché pour vendre le lait. Alors qu'elle faisait des pas vers le marché, ses pensées ont fait des pas vers la richesse. En chemin, elle n'arrêtait pas de penser à l'argent qu'elle gagnerait en vendant le lait. Puis elle réfléchit à ce qu'elle ferait de cet argent.

Elle se parlait à elle-même et disait : « Une fois que j'aurai l'argent, j'achèterai un poulet. La poule pondra des œufs et j'aurai plus de poules. Ils pondront tous des œufs et je les vendrai plus cher. Ensuite, j'achèterai la maison sur la colline et tout le monde m'enviera. Elle était très heureuse d'être bientôt très riche. Avec ces pensées heureuses, elle marcha en avant. Mais soudain, elle a trébuché et est tombée. Les deux seaux de lait sont tombés et tous ses rêves ont été brisés. Le lait s'est répandu sur le sol et tout ce que Patty pouvait faire était de pleurer. « Plus de rêve, cria-t-elle bêtement !

The Milkmaid and Her Pail (Spanish)
La lechera y su balde
Patty, una lechera, ordeñaba a su vaca y tenía dos cubos llenos de leche fresca y cremosa. Puso los dos cubos de leche en un palo y se dirigió al mercado a vender la leche. Mientras avanzaba hacia el mercado, sus pensamientos daban pasos hacia la riqueza. En su camino, no dejaba de pensar en el dinero que ganaría vendiendo la leche. Luego pensó en lo que haría con ese dinero.

Hablaba consigo misma y dijo: "Una vez que obtenga el dinero, compraré un pollo. La gallina pondrá huevos y yo conseguiré más gallinas. Todos pondrán huevos y los venderé por más dinero. Entonces, compraré la casa en la colina y todos me envidiarán ". Estaba muy feliz de que pronto sería muy rica. Con estos pensamientos felices, marchó adelante. Pero de repente, tropezó y cayó. Ambos cubos de leche cayeron y todos sus sueños se hicieron añicos. La leche se derramó por el suelo y lo único que pudo hacer Patty fue llorar. "¡No más sueños," gritó tontamente!

The Milkmaid and Her Pail (German)
Die Milchmagd und ihr Eimer

Patty, eine Melkerin, melkte ihre Kuh und hatte zwei volle Eimer mit frischer, cremiger Milch. Sie stellte beide Eimer Milch auf einen Stock und machte sich auf den Weg zum Markt, um die Milch zu verkaufen. Als sie Schritte in Richtung Markt machte, gingen ihre Gedanken Schritte in Richtung Reichtum. Unterwegs dachte sie immer wieder an das Geld, das sie mit dem Verkauf der Milch verdienen würde. Dann überlegte sie, was sie mit dem Geld machen würde.

Sie sprach mit sich selbst und sagte: „Sobald ich das Geld habe, kaufe ich ein Huhn. Das Huhn wird Eier legen und ich werde mehr Hühner bekommen. Sie werden alle Eier legen und ich werde sie für mehr Geld verkaufen. Dann kaufe ich das Haus auf dem Hügel und alle werden mich beneiden." Sie war sehr froh, dass sie bald sehr reich sein würde. Mit diesen glücklichen Gedanken marschierte sie voran. Doch plötzlich stolperte sie und stürzte. Beide Eimer mit der Milch fielen und alle ihre Träume wurden zerschmettert. Die Milch tropfte auf den Boden, und Patty konnte nur weinen. „Kein Traum mehr", rief sie töricht!

Lesson 23

Story Speaking

The Proud Rose (English)

Once upon a time, there was a beautiful rose plant in a garden. One rose flower on the plant was proud of its beauty. However, it was disappointed that it was growing next to an ugly cactus. Every day, the rose would insult the cactus about its looks, but the cactus stayed quiet. All the other plants in the garden tried to stop the rose from bullying the cactus, but the rose was too swayed by its own beauty to listen to anyone.

One summer, a well in the garden dried up and there was no water for the plants. The rose slowly began to wilt. The rose saw a sparrow dip its beak into the cactus for some water. The rose then felt ashamed for having made fun of the cactus all this time. But because it was in need of water, it went to ask the cactus if it could have some water. The kind cactus agreed, and they both got through summer as friends.

The Proud Rose (French)
La Rose fière
Il était une fois un magnifique rosier dans un jardin. Une fleur de rose sur la plante était fière de sa beauté. Cependant, il était déçu qu'il pousse à côté d'un cactus laid. Chaque jour, la rose insultait le cactus à cause de son apparence, mais le cactus restait silencieux. Toutes les autres plantes du jardin ont essayé d'empêcher la rose d'intimider le cactus, mais la rose était trop influencée par sa propre beauté pour écouter qui que ce soit.

Un été, un puits dans le jardin s'est asséché et il n'y avait plus d'eau pour les plantes. La rose commença lentement à se faner. La rose a vu un moineau plonger son bec dans le cactus pour de l'eau. La rose eut alors honte de s'être moquée du cactus pendant tout ce temps. Mais comme il avait besoin d'eau, il alla demander au cactus s'il pouvait avoir de l'eau. Le gentil cactus a accepté, et ils ont tous les deux traversé l'été en tant qu'amis.

The Proud Rose (Spanish)
La orgullosa rosa

Érase una vez, una hermosa planta de rosas en un jardín. Una rosa de la planta estaba orgullosa de su belleza. Sin embargo, estaba decepcionado de que estuviera creciendo junto a un cactus feo. Todos los días, la rosa insultaba al cactus por su apariencia, pero el cactus se quedaba callado. Todas las otras plantas en el jardín intentaron evitar que la rosa intimidara al cactus, pero la rosa estaba demasiado influenciada por su propia belleza como para escuchar a nadie.

Un verano, un pozo en el jardín se secó y no había agua para las plantas. La rosa comenzó a marchitarse lentamente. La rosa vio a un gorrión sumergir su pico en el cactus para beber un poco de agua. La rosa se sintió avergonzada por haberse burlado del cactus todo este tiempo. Pero como necesitaba agua, fue a preguntarle al cactus si podía tener un poco de agua. El amable cactus estuvo de acuerdo, y ambos pasaron el verano como amigos.

The Proud Rose (German)
Die stolze Rose

Es war einmal eine schöne Rosenpflanze in einem Garten. Eine Rosenblüte an der Pflanze war stolz auf ihre Schönheit. Es war jedoch enttäuscht, dass es neben einem hässlichen Kaktus wuchs. Jeden Tag beleidigte die Rose den Kaktus wegen seines Aussehens, aber der Kaktus blieb ruhig. Alle anderen Pflanzen im Garten versuchten, die Rose davon abzuhalten, den Kaktus zu schikanieren, aber die Rose war zu sehr von ihrer eigenen Schönheit beeinflusst, um auf irgendjemanden zu hören.

Eines Sommers trocknete ein Brunnen im Garten aus und es gab kein Wasser für die Pflanzen. Die Rose begann langsam zu welken. Die Rose sah, wie ein Spatz seinen Schnabel in den Kaktus tauchte, um etwas Wasser zu holen. Die Rose schämte sich dann dafür, dass sie sich die ganze Zeit über den Kaktus lustig gemacht hatte. Aber weil er Wasser brauchte, fragte er den Kaktus, ob er etwas Wasser haben könnte. Der freundliche Kaktus stimmte zu und beide kamen als Freunde durch den Sommer.

Lesson 24

Story Speaking

A Bundle of Sticks (English)
Once upon a time, three neighbours living in a village were having trouble with their crops. Each of the neighbours had one field, but the crops on their fields were infested with pests and were wilting. Every day, they would come up with different ideas to help their crops. The first one tried using a scarecrow in his field, the second used pesticides, and the third built a fence on his field, all to no avail.

One day, the village head came by and called the three farmers. He gave them each a stick and asked them to break it. The farmers could break them easily. He then gave them a bundle of three sticks, and again, asked them to break it. This time, the farmers struggled to break the sticks. The village head said, "Together, you are stronger and work better than you do it alone." The farmers understood what the village head was saying. They pooled in their resources and got rid of the pests from their fields.

A Bundle of Sticks (French)
Un paquet de bâtons

Il était une fois trois voisins vivant dans un village qui avaient des problèmes avec leurs récoltes. Chacun des voisins avait un champ, mais les cultures sur leurs champs étaient infestées de parasites et se fanaient. Chaque jour, ils proposaient des idées différentes pour aider leurs cultures. Le premier a essayé d'utiliser un épouvantail dans son champ, le second a utilisé des pesticides et le troisième a construit une clôture sur son champ, en vain.

Un jour, le chef du village est passé et a appelé les trois agriculteurs. Il leur a donné à chacun un bâton et leur a demandé de le casser. Les agriculteurs pourraient les casser facilement. Il leur a ensuite donné un paquet de trois bâtons, et encore une fois, leur a demandé de le casser. Cette fois, les agriculteurs ont eu du mal à casser les bâtons. Le chef du village a dit : « Ensemble, vous êtes plus forts et travaillez mieux que seul. » Les agriculteurs ont compris ce que disait le chef du village. Ils ont mis en commun leurs ressources et se sont débarrassés des parasites de leurs champs.

A Bundle of Sticks (Spanish)
Un paquete de palos

Érase una vez, tres vecinos que vivían en un pueblo tenían problemas con sus cultivos. Cada uno de los vecinos tenía un campo, pero los cultivos de sus campos estaban infestados de plagas y se estaban marchitando. Todos los días, se les ocurrían diferentes ideas para ayudar a sus cultivos. El primero intentó usar un espantapájaros en su campo, el segundo usó pesticidas y el tercero construyó una cerca en su campo, todo fue en vano.

Un día, el jefe de la aldea se acercó y llamó a los tres agricultores. Les dio a cada uno un palo y les pidió que lo rompieran. Los agricultores podrían romperlos fácilmente. Luego les dio un paquete de tres palos y, nuevamente, les pidió que lo rompieran. Esta vez, los agricultores lucharon por romper los palos. El jefe de la aldea dijo: "Juntos, son más fuertes y trabajan mejor que si lo hacen solo". Los agricultores entendieron lo que decía el jefe de la aldea. Reunieron sus recursos y eliminaron las plagas de sus campos.

A Bundle of Sticks (German)
Ein Bündel Stöcke

Es waren einmal drei Nachbarn, die in einem Dorf lebten, hatten Probleme mit ihrer Ernte. Jeder der Nachbarn hatte ein Feld, aber die Ernte auf ihren Feldern war von Schädlingen befallen und verwelkte. Jeden Tag kamen sie auf verschiedene Ideen, um ihren Pflanzen zu helfen. Der erste versuchte, auf seinem Feld eine Vogelscheuche einzusetzen, der zweite verwendete Pestizide und der dritte baute einen Zaun auf seinem Feld, alles ohne Erfolg.

Eines Tages kam der Dorfvorsteher vorbei und rief die drei Bauern. Er gab ihnen jedem einen Stock und forderte sie auf, ihn zu zerbrechen. Die Bauern könnten sie leicht zerbrechen. Dann gab er ihnen ein Bündel mit drei Stöcken und forderte sie erneut auf, es zu zerbrechen. Diesmal hatten die Bauern Mühe, die Stöcke zu zerbrechen. Der Dorfvorsteher sagte: „Gemeinsam seid ihr stärker und arbeitet besser als alleine." Die Bauern verstanden, was der Dorfvorsteher sagte. Sie bündelten ihre Ressourcen und beseitigten die Schädlinge von ihren Feldern.

Lesson 25

Story Speaking

The Ant and the Dove (English)
On a hot day of summer, an ant was walking in search of water. After walking around for some time, she saw a river and was delighted to see it. She climbed up on a small rock to drink the water, but she slipped and fell into the river. She was drowning but a dove who was sitting on a nearby tree helped her. Seeing the ant in trouble, the dove quickly dropped a leaf into the water. The ant moved towards the leaf and climbed up on it. The dove then carefully pulled the leaf out and placed it on the land. This way, the ant's life was saved and she was forever indebted to the dove. The ant and the dove became the best of friends and days passed happily. However, one day, a hunter arrived at the forest. He saw the beautiful dove sitting on the tree and aimed his gun at the dove. The ant, who was saved the dove saw this and bit on the heel of the hunter. He shouted from the pain and dropped the gun. The dove was alarmed by the voice of the hunter and realised what could have happened with him. He flew away!

The Ant and the Dove (French)
La fourmi et la colombe

Par une chaude journée d'été, une fourmi marchait à la recherche d'eau. Après avoir marché quelque temps, elle a vu une rivière et a été ravie de la voir. Elle a grimpé sur un petit rocher pour boire l'eau, mais elle a glissé et est tombée dans la rivière. Elle se noyait mais une colombe assise sur un arbre voisin l'a aidée. Voyant la fourmi en difficulté, la colombe laissa rapidement tomber une feuille dans l'eau. La fourmi se dirigea vers la feuille et grimpa dessus. La colombe a ensuite soigneusement retiré la feuille et l'a placée sur la terre. De cette façon, la vie de la fourmi a été sauvée et elle était à jamais redevable à la colombe. La fourmi et la colombe devinrent les meilleures amies et les jours passèrent joyeusement. Cependant, un jour, un chasseur est arrivé dans la forêt. Il a vu la belle colombe assise sur l'arbre et a pointé son arme sur la colombe. La fourmi, qui a sauvé la colombe, a vu cela et a mordu le talon du chasseur. Il a crié de douleur et a laissé tomber le pistolet. La colombe fut alarmée par la voix du chasseur et réalisa ce qui avait pu lui arriver. Il s'est envolé!

The Ant and the Dove (Spanish)
La hormiga y la paloma

En un caluroso día de verano, una hormiga caminaba en busca de agua. Después de caminar un rato, vio un río y se alegró de verlo. Se subió a una pequeña roca para beber el agua, pero resbaló y cayó al río. Se estaba ahogando, pero una paloma que estaba sentada en un árbol cercano la ayudó. Al ver a la hormiga en problemas, la paloma rápidamente dejó caer una hoja al agua. La hormiga se acercó a la hoja y se subió a ella. Luego, la paloma sacó con cuidado la hoja y la colocó en la tierra. De esta manera, se salvó la vida de la hormiga y quedó en deuda con la paloma para siempre. La hormiga y la paloma se convirtieron en las mejores amigas y los días pasaron felices. Sin embargo, un día llegó un cazador al bosque. Vio a la hermosa paloma sentada en el árbol y apuntó con su arma a la paloma. La hormiga, que se salvó de la paloma vio esto y mordió el talón del cazador. Gritó de dolor y dejó caer el arma. La paloma se alarmó por la voz del cazador y se dio cuenta de lo que pudo haber pasado con él. ¡Se fue volando!

The Ant and the Dove (German)
Die Ameise und die Taube

An einem heißen Sommertag ging eine Ameise auf der Suche nach Wasser. Nachdem sie einige Zeit herumgelaufen war, sah sie einen Fluss und freute sich, ihn zu sehen. Sie kletterte auf einen kleinen Felsen, um das Wasser zu trinken, aber sie rutschte aus und fiel in den Fluss. Sie ertrank, aber eine Taube, die auf einem nahen Baum saß, half ihr. Als die Taube die Ameise in Schwierigkeiten sah, ließ sie schnell ein Blatt ins Wasser fallen. Die Ameise ging auf das Blatt zu und kletterte darauf. Dann zog die Taube das Blatt vorsichtig heraus und legte es auf das Land.Auf diese Weise wurde das Leben der Ameise gerettet und sie war der Taube für immer zu Dank verpflichtet. Die Ameise und die Taube wurden die besten Freunde und die Tage vergingen glücklich. Eines Tages kam jedoch ein Jäger im Wald an. Er sah die schöne Taube auf dem Baum sitzen und zielte mit seiner Waffe auf die Taube. Die Ameise, die die Taube gerettet hatte, sah dies und biss dem Jäger in die Ferse. Er schrie vor Schmerz und ließ die Waffe fallen. Die Taube war von der Stimme des Jägers alarmiert und erkannte, was mit ihm passiert sein könnte. Er ist weggeflogen!

Lesson 26

Story Speaking

The Fox and the Grapes (English)
On a hot summer day, a fox wandered across the jungle in order to get some food. He was very hungry and desperately in search of food. He searched everywhere, but couldn't find anything that he could eat. His stomach was rumbling and his search continued. Soon he reached a vineyard which was laden with juicy grapes. The fox looked around to check if he was safe from the hunters. No one was around, so he decided to steal some grapes. He jumped high and high, but he couldn't reach the grapes. The grapes were too high but he refused to give up. The fox jumped high in the air to catch the grapes in his mouth, but he missed. He tried once more but missed again. He tried a few more times, but couldn't reach. It was getting dark and the fox was getting angry. His legs hurt, so he gave up in the end. Walking away, he said, "I'm sure the grapes were sour anyway."

The Fox and the Grapes (French)
Le Renard et les Raisins

Par une chaude journée d'été, un renard a erré à travers la jungle afin d'obtenir de la nourriture. Il avait très faim et cherchait désespérément de la nourriture. Il a cherché partout, mais n'a rien trouvé à manger. Son estomac gargouillait et sa recherche continuait. Bientôt, il atteignit un vignoble chargé de raisins juteux. Le renard regarda autour de lui pour vérifier s'il était à l'abri des chasseurs. Personne n'était là, alors il a décidé de voler des raisins. Il a sauté haut et haut, mais il ne pouvait pas atteindre les raisins. Les raisins étaient trop hauts mais il refusa d'abandonner. Le renard a sauté haut dans les airs pour attraper les raisins dans sa bouche, mais il a raté. Il a essayé une fois de plus mais a raté à nouveau. Il a essayé plusieurs fois, mais n'a pas pu atteindre. Il commençait à faire sombre et le renard s'énervait. Ses jambes lui faisaient mal, alors il a finalement abandonné. En s'éloignant, il a dit: "Je suis sûr que les raisins étaient aigres de toute façon."

The Fox and the Grapes (Spanish)
El zorro y las uvas

En un caluroso día de verano, un zorro deambulaba por la jungla para conseguir algo de comida. Tenía mucha hambre y buscaba desesperadamente comida. Buscó por todas partes, pero no pudo encontrar nada que pudiera comer. Su estómago retumbaba y su búsqueda continuó. Pronto llegó a un viñedo cargado de jugosas uvas. El zorro miró a su alrededor para comprobar si estaba a salvo de los cazadores. No había nadie cerca, así que decidió robar algunas uvas. Saltó alto y alto, pero no pudo alcanzar las uvas. Las uvas estaban demasiado altas pero se negó a darse por vencido. El zorro saltó alto en el aire para atrapar las uvas con la boca, pero falló. Lo intentó una vez más, pero falló de nuevo. Lo intentó unas cuantas veces más, pero no pudo alcanzar. Estaba oscureciendo y el zorro se estaba enojando. Le dolían las piernas, por lo que se rindió al final. Al alejarse, dijo: "Estoy seguro de que las uvas estaban agrias de todos modos".

The Fox and the Grapes (German)
Der Fuchs und die Trauben

An einem heißen Sommertag wanderte ein Fuchs durch den Dschungel, um etwas zu essen zu bekommen. Er war sehr hungrig und suchte verzweifelt nach Nahrung. Er suchte überall, fand aber nichts, was er essen konnte. Sein Magen knurrte und seine Suche ging weiter. Bald erreichte er einen Weinberg, der mit saftigen Trauben beladen war. Der Fuchs sah sich um, um zu sehen, ob er vor den Jägern sicher war. Niemand war in der Nähe, also beschloss er, ein paar Trauben zu stehlen. Er sprang hoch und hoch, aber er konnte die Trauben nicht erreichen. Die Trauben waren zu hoch, aber er weigerte sich, aufzugeben. Der Fuchs sprang hoch in die Luft, um die Trauben mit seinem Maul aufzufangen, aber er verfehlte. Er versuchte es noch einmal, verfehlte aber wieder. Er versuchte es noch ein paar Mal, aber er konnte nicht erreichen. Es wurde dunkel und der Fuchs wurde wütend. Seine Beine taten weh, also gab er am Ende auf. Als er wegging, sagte er: "Ich bin mir sicher, dass die Trauben sowieso sauer waren."

Lesson 27

Story Speaking

The Bear and Two Friends (English)
One day, two best friends were walking on a lonely and dangerous path through a jungle. As the sun began to set, they grew afraid but held on to each other. Suddenly, they saw a bear in their path. One of the boys ran to the nearest tree and climbed it in a jiffy. The other boy did not know how to climb the tree by himself, so he lay on the ground, pretending to be dead. The bear approached the boy on the ground and sniffed around his head. After appearing to whisper something in the boy's ear, the bear went on its way. The boy on the tree climbed down and asked his friend what the bear had whispered in his ear. He replied, "Do not trust friends who do not care for you."

The Bear and Two Friends (French)
L'ours et ses deux amis

Un jour, deux meilleurs amis marchaient sur un chemin solitaire et dangereux à travers une jungle. Alors que le soleil commençait à se coucher, ils ont eu peur mais se sont accrochés l'un à l'autre. Soudain, ils virent un ours sur leur chemin. L'un des garçons a couru jusqu'à l'arbre le plus proche et l'a grimpé en un tournemain. L'autre garçon ne savait pas comment grimper à l'arbre tout seul, alors il s'est allongé sur le sol, faisant semblant d'être mort. L'ours s'approcha du garçon au sol et renifla autour de sa tête. Après avoir semblé murmurer quelque chose à l'oreille du garçon, l'ours continua son chemin. Le garçon sur l'arbre est descendu et a demandé à son ami ce que l'ours avait chuchoté à son oreille. Il a répondu : " Ne fais pas confiance à des amis qui ne se soucient pas de toi."

The Bear and Two Friends (Spanish)
El oso y dos amigos

Un día, dos mejores amigos caminaban por un sendero solitario y peligroso a través de la jungla. Cuando el sol comenzó a ponerse, se asustaron, pero se abrazaron el uno al otro. De repente, vieron un oso en su camino. Uno de los chicos corrió hacia el árbol más cercano y se subió en un santiamén. El otro niño no sabía cómo trepar al árbol por sí mismo, así que se tumbó en el suelo, fingiendo estar muerto. El oso se acercó al niño en el suelo y olisqueó alrededor de su cabeza. Después de parecer susurrar algo al oído del niño, el oso siguió su camino. El niño del árbol se bajó y le preguntó a su amigo qué le había susurrado el oso al oído. Él respondió: "No confíes en los amigos que no se preocupan por ti".

The Bear and Two Friends (German)
Der Bär und zwei Freunde

Eines Tages gingen zwei beste Freunde auf einem einsamen und gefährlichen Pfad durch einen Dschungel. Als die Sonne unterging, bekamen sie Angst, hielten aber aneinander fest. Plötzlich sahen sie einen Bären auf ihrem Weg. Einer der Jungen rannte zum nächsten Baum und kletterte im Handumdrehen darauf. Der andere Junge wusste nicht, wie er alleine auf den Baum klettern sollte, also lag er auf dem Boden und gab vor, tot zu sein. Der Bär näherte sich dem Jungen am Boden und schnupperte an seinem Kopf herum. Nachdem er dem Jungen scheinbar etwas ins Ohr geflüstert hatte, machte sich der Bär auf den Weg. Der Junge auf dem Baum kletterte herunter und fragte seinen Freund, was ihm der Bär ins Ohr geflüstert habe. Er antwortete: "Vertraue keinen Freunden, die sich nicht um dich kümmern."

Lesson 28

Story Speaking

Friends Forever (English)
Once upon a time, there lived a mouse and a frog, who were the best of friends. Every morning, the frog would hop out of the pond to visit the mouse, who lived inside the hole of the tree. He would spend time with the mouse and go back home. One day, the frog realised that he was making too much of an effort to visit the mouse while the mouse never came to meet him at the pond. This made him angry, and he decided to make things right by forcefully taking him to his house.

When the mouse wasn't looking, the frog tied a string to the mouse's tail and tied the other end to his own leg, and hopped away. The mouse started getting dragged with him. Then, the frog jumped into the pond to swim. However, when he looked back, he saw that the mouse had started to drown and was struggling to breathe! The frog quickly untied the string from his tail and took him to the shore. Seeing the mouse with his eyes barely open made the frog very sad, and he immediately regretted pulling him into the pond.

Friends Forever (French)
Amis pour toujours

Il était une fois une souris et une grenouille, qui étaient les meilleures amies. Chaque matin, la grenouille sautait hors de l'étang pour rendre visite à la souris, qui vivait dans le trou de l'arbre. Il passait du temps avec la souris et rentrait chez lui. Un jour, la grenouille s'est rendu compte qu'il faisait trop d'efforts pour rendre visite à la souris alors que la souris n'est jamais venue le rencontrer à l'étang. Cela l'a mis en colère et il a décidé d'arranger les choses en l'emmenant de force chez lui.

Lorsque la souris ne regardait pas, la grenouille a attaché une ficelle à la queue de la souris et a attaché l'autre extrémité à sa propre jambe, et a sauté. La souris a commencé à être traînée avec lui. Ensuite, la grenouille a sauté dans l'étang pour nager. Cependant, quand il a regardé en arrière, il a vu que la souris avait commencé à se noyer et avait du mal à respirer ! La grenouille a rapidement détaché la ficelle de sa queue et l'a emmené sur le rivage. Voir la souris avec ses yeux à peine ouverts a rendu la grenouille très triste, et il a immédiatement regretté de l'avoir entraîné dans l'étang.

Friends Forever (Spanish)
Amigos por siempre

Érase una vez, un ratón y una rana, que eran los mejores amigos. Todas las mañanas, la rana saltaba del estanque para visitar al ratón, que vivía dentro del agujero del árbol. Pasaría tiempo con el ratón y volvería a casa. Un día, la rana se dio cuenta de que estaba haciendo un gran esfuerzo para visitar al ratón, mientras que el ratón nunca llegó a encontrarse con él en el estanque. Esto lo enfureció y decidió arreglar las cosas llevándolo a la fuerza a su casa.

Cuando el ratón no miraba, la rana ató una cuerda a la cola del ratón, ató el otro extremo a su propia pierna y saltó. El ratón empezó a ser arrastrado con él. Luego, la rana saltó al estanque para nadar. Sin embargo, cuando miró hacia atrás, vio que el ratón había comenzado a ahogarse y ¡estaba luchando por respirar! La rana rápidamente desató la cuerda de su cola y lo llevó a la orilla. Ver al ratón con los ojos apenas abiertos entristeció mucho a la rana, e inmediatamente se arrepintió de haberlo llevado al estanque.

Friends Forever (German)
Für immer Freunde

Es waren einmal eine Maus und ein Frosch, die die besten Freunde waren. Jeden Morgen hüpfte der Frosch aus dem Teich, um die Maus zu besuchen, die im Loch des Baumes lebte. Er würde Zeit mit der Maus verbringen und nach Hause zurückkehren. Eines Tages merkte der Frosch, dass er sich zu sehr bemühte, die Maus zu besuchen, während die Maus ihn nie am Teich abholte. Das machte ihn wütend und er beschloss, die Dinge in Ordnung zu bringen, indem er ihn gewaltsam in sein Haus brachte.

Als die Maus nicht hinsah, band der Frosch eine Schnur an den Schwanz der Maus und band das andere Ende an sein eigenes Bein und hüpfte davon. Die Maus fing an, mit ihm gezogen zu werden. Dann sprang der Frosch in den Teich, um zu schwimmen. Als er jedoch zurückblickte, sah er, dass die Maus zu ertrinken begann und Schwierigkeiten hatte zu atmen! Der Frosch löste schnell die Schnur von seinem Schwanz und brachte ihn ans Ufer. Die Maus mit kaum geöffneten Augen zu sehen, machte den Frosch sehr traurig und er bereute es sofort, ihn in den Teich gezogen zu haben.

Cromosys

Education and Technology Research Center
Registered with Govt. of India
Twenty years of experience
+91-9561450045
Nallasopara (W), Mumbai, India
https://www.facebook.com/cromosys

Cromosys Publication

Foreign Languages Conversation

French – Spanish – German – English

Niranjan Jha Showman

NIRANJAN JHA SHOWMAN

Founder - Niranjan Jha Showman

Education and Technology Research Center

Patankar Park, Nallasopara (W), Mumbai. +91-9561450045

Education, Technology, Publication, Healthcare, Newsmedia, Realtor, Filmmaking

www.facebook.com/cromosys

Cromosys Publication
Teach
Yourself
German
NIRANJAN JHA SHOWMAN

Cromosys Publication
Teach
Yourself
French
NIRANJAN JHA SHOWMAN

Cromosys Publication
Teach
Yourself
Spanish
NIRANJAN JHA SHOWMAN

Cromosys Publication

English Voice Accent and Pronunciation

NIRANJAN JHA SHOWMAN

Teach
Yourself
Autodesk
MAYA
Cromosys Publication
NIRANJAN JHA SHOWMAN

Cromosys Publication
Teach
Yourself
Autodesk
3ds Max
NIRANJAN JHA SHOWMAN

Cromosys Publication
CRIMINAL FACTORY
NIRANJAN JHA SHOWMAN

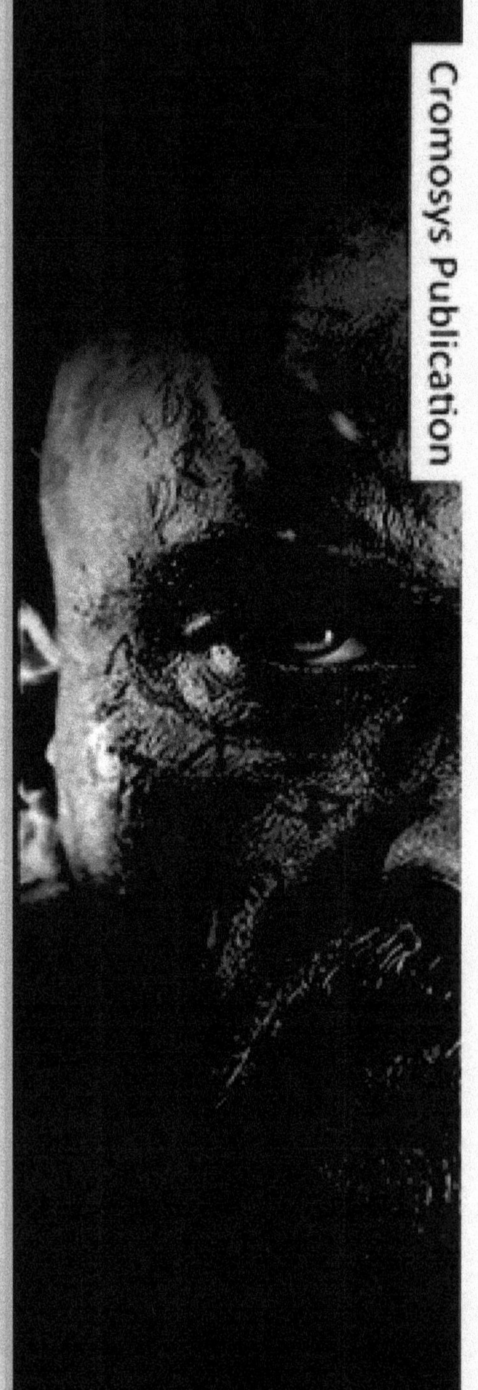

Cromosys Publication
FOCAL DISASTER
NIRANJAN JHA SHOWMAN

Cromosys Publication
Your talents will not help you succeed
without your skill of using them.
NIRANJAN JHA SHOWMAN
BE
MILLIONAIRE
LIKE
ME

Copyright Office
Government of India

सत्यमेव जयते

Extracts
from the Register
of Copyrights

Dated : 20/08/2022

1.	Registration Number	:	**T-98582-2022**
2.	Name, address and nationality of the applicant	:	NIRANJAN JHA SHOWMAN, CROMOSYS PUBLICATION, 001, JAYSATYAM, PATANKAR ROAD, NALLASOPARA (W), MUMBAI, MAHARASHTRA - 401203. INDIAN
3.	Nature of the applicant's interest in the copyright of the work	:	AUTHOR
4.	Class and description of the work	:	LITERARY / BOOK
5.	Title of the work	:	**FOREIGN LANGUAGES CONVERSATION**
6.	Language of the work	:	ENGLISH
7.	Name, address and nationality of the author and if the author is deceased, date of his decease	:	NIRANJAN JHA SHOWMAN, CROMOSYS PUBLICATION, 001, JAYSATYAM, PATANKAR ROAD, NALLASOPARA (W), MUMBAI, MAHARASHTRA - 401203. INDIAN
8.	Whether the work is published or unpublished	:	UNPUBLISHED
9.	Year and country of first publication and name, address and nationality of the publisher	:	N.A.
10.	Years and countries of subsequent publications, if any, and names, addresses and nationalities of the publishers	:	N.A. SAME AS ABOVE
11.	Names, addresses and nationalities of the owners of various rights comprising the copyright in the work and the extent of rights held by each, together with particulars of assignments and licences, if any	:	
12.	Names, addresses and nationalities of other persons, if any, authorised to assign or licence of rights comprising the copyright	:	N.A.
13.	If the work is an 'Artistic work', the location of the original work, including name, address and nationality of the person in possession of the work. (In the case of an architectural work, the year of completion of the work should also be shown).	:	N.A.
14.	If the work is an 'Artistic work', whether it is registered under the Designs Act 2000 if yes give details.	:	N.A.
15.	If the work is an 'Artistic work', capable of being registered as a design under the Designs Act 2000.whether it has been applied to an article though an industrial process and ,if yes ,the number of times it is reproduced.	:	N.A.
16.	Remarks, if any	:	

Diary Number :   9753/2020-DF/T
Date of Application : 12/08/2021
Date of Receipt :   12/08/2021

DEPUTY REGISTRAR OF COPYRIGHTS